Studies in O
History

Jesse Lyman Hurlbut

Alpha Editions

This edition published in 2024

ISBN : 9789364732918

Design and Setting By
Alpha Editions
www.alphaedis.com
Email - info@alphaedis.com

As per information held with us this book is in Public Domain.
This book is a reproduction of an important historical work. Alpha Editions uses the best technology to reproduce historical work in the same manner it was first published to preserve its original nature. Any marks or number seen are left intentionally to preserve its true form.

Contents

PREFACE. ....- 1 -

HINTS TO STUDENTS. ....- 4 -

HINTS TO TEACHERS. ....- 6 -

THE COURSE DIVIDED INTO
LESSONS. ....- 7 -

First Study. THE BEGINNINGS OF BIBLE
HISTORY. ....- 10 -

Second Study. THE WANDERING IN THE
WILDERNESS. ....- 17 -

Third Study. THE CONQUEST OF
CANAAN. ....- 25 -

Fourth Study. THE AGE OF THE
HEROES. ....- 31 -

Fifth Study. THE RISE OF THE
ISRAELITE EMPIRE. ....- 38 -

Sixth Study. THE GOLDEN AGE OF
ISRAEL ....- 44 -

Seventh Study. THE RIVAL THRONES.—
ISRAEL..- 50 -

Eighth Study. THE RIVAL THRONES—
JUDAH. ....- 57 -

Ninth Study. THE CAPTIVITY OF
JUDAH. ....- 62 -

Tenth Study. The Jewish Province...- 71 -

PREFACE.

THE New Testament is the outgrowth and development of the Old. There is no revelation in the gospels or the epistles which is not in its essence contained in the elder Scripture; though to make it manifest required the incarnation of God's Son and the descent of the Holy Spirit. Therefore, to understand the New Testament it is necessary to study the Old Testament. We cannot appreciate Matthew's point of view of Christ as the Messiah until we have looked upon the throne of David, and Solomon in all his glory; the theology of Paul is blind until read in the light of Moses and Isaiah; and Hebrews will obtain a new meaning when placed side by side with Leviticus. Every chapter in the New Testament has its references to parallel passages in the Old Testament.

When we open the Old Testament we find it, first of all, a book of history. We are apt to look upon the Bible as a dictionary of doctrine, wherein we are to search for sentences as proof-texts. But instead it contains the story of redemption in the form of a history. We see how God chose a family and pruned off its dead branches and caused it to grow into a nation; then, how he trained and disciplined that nation through fifteen centuries, until upon it blossomed the Divine Man. The history of the Bible is the history of humanity, of literature, of ethics, of religion, of doctrine; and no one who studies it carefully will fail of an abundant reward for his endeavor.

In most works upon Bible history the purpose of the author seems to be merely to arrange in chronological order a series of events without much regard to their importance or their relations to each other. The successive reigns of kings, the chronicles of courts, the reports of battles form the contents of most histories, whether sacred or secular. Works like these have their value in the statement of those facts which form the basis and working material of history. But mere facts chronologically arranged do not constitute a history, any more than words alphabetically arranged constitute a literature. True history records processes, the relation of cause and effect, the formative influences and their result in national life. The true history of England shows not annals of kings and achievements of warriors, but the development of a mighty people. The true history of Greece gives the secret springs of that intense activity which in two centuries called forth more great men in more departments of life than all the rest of the world could produce in a thousand years. The true history of Israel—which is the history of the Old Testament—shows how a little people in their mountain-eyrie grew up to a destiny more glorious than that of the proudest empire of all the earth, the honor of giving religion to mankind.

The aim of this little book is to present the outlines of that remarkable history of the chosen people. What their mission was, how they were trained for it, and how the world was prepared to receive it together constitute the three threads woven together in this work. It is a book of outlines to be studied, not of chapters to be read. The reader will doubtless find the paragraphs somewhat disconnected, but we trust that the student may receive from them suggestions for thought.

In the preparation of this book many works have been read and examined; but it is not my purpose to give a catalogue of them. I would name, however, a very few books which will be of service to the student, and will be almost a necessity for the teacher who expects to use these outlines in the class, for one secret of successful teaching is for the teacher to have at his command a fund of knowledge vastly greater than that contained in the text-book. For this purpose the following works are named, none of which are too abstruse or difficult for the average reader:

1. *Outline of Bible History.* Bishop J. F. Hurst. A small book, containing merely the facts of the subject.

2. *Old Testament History.* William Smith. A larger work and valuable, but ending with the Old Testament canon. An additional chapter on the interval between Old and New Testament history would greatly improve the book.

3. *Lectures on the History of the Jewish Church.* Dean A. P. Stanley. Three large volumes, in a brilliant but diffuse style, advanced to the knowledge of twenty years ago; not altogether sound in its critical point of view, yet to be read by all who would understand the subject.

4. *Hours with the Bible.* Cunningham Geikie. Six volumes, discussing Bible history in all of its aspects, particularly in its relations with secular history. Perhaps this is the best work on the subject for the reader who is not a specialist. But it is prolix, and could be compressed to advantage.

There is need, in my opinion, of a good semi-popular Bible history, in one volume or two, to present results rather than processes of thought, and to embody all the latest knowledge from the study of the Scriptures and the monuments of the ancient world.

It is needless to urge upon the student that the best book for the study of Bible history is the Bible itself. The historical books should be read with great care, even to their details of genealogical tables. The most valuable document in the study of the origin of races is the tenth chapter of Genesis; and a catalogue of names in the opening of Chronicles will give a clew to the chronology of the sojourn in Egypt. The prophetical books will aid the student, and the Psalms will irradiate certain dark periods. Whoever undertakes to use these outlines should examine every text cited for its suggestion upon the subject.

This book is commended to Bible students, to Sunday-school normal classes, and to all who love the word, with a hope that it may be of service in calling attention to the Old Testament, and that it may lead some through the Old to enter into a better spiritual understanding of the New.

JESSE L. HURLBUT.

HINTS TO STUDENTS.

Those who desire merely to *read* this book or to look it over will not find it interesting. Those who already know how to study will not need these hints, and can use the book in their own way. But there are many who desire to study these subjects carefully, and yet do not know precisely how to do the work. For these students, earnest but untrained, the hints are given.

1. These studies should be pursued with the Bible close at hand, so that every Scripture reference may be at once searched out and read.

2. Begin each lesson by a general view; reading it through carefully, and memorizing the leading divisions of the outline, which are indicated by the Roman numerals I, II, III, etc. This will give the general plan of the lesson.

3. Now take up Part I of the lesson in detail; notice and memorize its subdivisions, indicated by 1, 2, 3, etc., and search out the Scripture references cited in it. If practicable, write out on a sheet of paper the reference (not the language of the text in full), and what each reference shows. Thus, with the references in the First Study, page 17, Part I:

BEGINNINGS OF BIBLE HISTORY. Part I. **Deluge.**

Gen. 7. Description of the flood.
Gen. 6. 5-7. God punished the world for wickedness.
Gen. 7. 23. Covered the inhabited earth.

4. It would be a good plan to write out in full, as a connected statement, all the facts in the section; thus: "The Bible says there was a deluge and the traditions of other nations attest it. The date commonly given is 2348 B. C. Its cause was God's anger with the wickedness of the race, and it covered the inhabited globe. God's purpose was to cleanse the world for a new epoch."

5. In like manner study out and write out all the facts obtained by a study of the lesson and the texts cited in it. This will greatly aid the memory in holding fast to the information gained.

6. Having done this, look at the blackboard outline at the end of the study, and see if you can read the outline of the lesson by the aid of the catch-words and indications which it affords. Study the lesson until you can read it with the blackboard outline, and then recall it without the outline.

7. Now read over the questions for review, one by one, and see if you can answer them. Do not cease your study until every question can be answered without the aid of the text.

8. Frequently review the lessons already learned. Before beginning the third study review the first and the second; before the fourth, review the first, second, and third, and at the completion of all the studies review them all. The knowledge gained by this thorough study will more than compensate for the time and trouble which it requires.

HINTS TO TEACHERS.

Classes may be organized on various plans and out of varied materials for the study of these lessons.

1. A teachers' class, composed of teachers, and also of senior scholars in the Sunday-school, may be formed to study the life of Christ, which is one of the most important subjects in the Bible. This may meet on an evening or an afternoon, and devote all the sessions to the study of the lesson, and to discussions upon it.

2. In many places a teachers' meeting is held for the study of the International Lesson, as a preparation for the Sunday-school class. A part of the time might be taken at this meeting for the study of these subjects. In that case it would be well to follow the division into lessons, as given on page 14.

3. A normal class may be organized among the brightest scholars in the Sunday-school, who should be trained to become teachers. This normal class may meet on an afternoon or an evening, or may take a lesson-period in the Sunday-school session.

4. These studies may be pursued by the young people's society of the church, or by a class formed under its auspices, meeting at such time and place as shall be found most convenient.

There are two methods in which these lessons may be taught: One is the *lecture method*, by which the instructor gives the lesson to the class in the form of a lecture, placing the outline upon the blackboard as he proceeds, calling upon the students to read the texts cited, and frequently reviewing the outline in a concert-drill. By this method the students may or may not have the books, as they and the instructor prefer. While it is not necessary to supply the class with the text-book, it will be a good plan to do so.

The other method, simpler and easier, is to let each student have a copy of the book, to expect the lesson to be prepared by the class, and to have it recited, either individually or in concert. Let each student gain all the information that he can upon the subject of the lesson; let each contribute his knowledge; let all talk freely, and all will be the gainers.

It would be a good plan to have papers read from time to time upon topics suggested by the course and parallel with it. A list of subjects for such special papers is given at the close of each study.

THE COURSE DIVIDED INTO LESSONS.

IN many places it will be found impracticable to give an entire evening to the study of these lessons. They may be taught at the close of the prayer-meeting, or of the young people's meeting, in short sections; or they may occupy a part of the hour at the weekly teachers' meeting for the study of the Sunday-school lesson; or they may be taught to the Normal class in the Sunday-school at the lesson hour. In the latter case, the regular lesson should receive some attention; and the members of the class should be expected to prepare it, and should be questioned upon it.

Often from twenty to thirty minutes is all that can be given in a class to studies like these. We have, therefore, divided the studies into short sections, each of which may be taught in about twenty minutes, if properly prepared by both teacher and students. Thus arranged, the course will be included in thirty-two lessons, as follows:

Lesson I.—*The Beginnings of Bible History.* The deluge and the dispersion. (First Study, I and II.)

Lesson II.—*The Beginnings of Bible History.* Rise of the empires, migration of Abraham, and journeys of the patriarchs. (First Study, III, IV, and V.)

Lesson III.—*The Beginnings of Bible History.* Sojourn in Egypt. (First Study, VI.) Also review First Study.

Lesson IV.—*The Wandering in the Wilderness.* Events leading to the wandering in the wilderness. (Second Study, I and II.)

Lesson V.—*The Wandering in the Wilderness.* Journeys of the wandering. (Second Study, III.)

Lesson VI.—*The Wandering in the Wilderness.* Results of the wandering. (Second Study IV.) Also review Second Study.

Lesson VII.—*The Conquest of Canaan.* Canaanites and campaigns of the conquest. (Third Study, I and II.)

Lesson VIII.—*The Conquest of Canaan.* Aspect of Israel after conquest. (Third Study, IV.) Also review Third Study.

Lesson IX.—*The Age of the Heroes.* Condition of Israel and the judges of Israel. (Fourth Study, I and II.)

Lesson X.—*The Age of the Heroes.* The oppressions and deliverers. (Fourth Study, III.)

Lesson XI.—*The Age of the Heroes.* General aspects of the period. (Fourth Study, IV.) Also review Fourth Study.

Lesson XII.—*The Rise of the Israelite Empire.* Causes leading to the monarchy, and character of the Israelite kingdom. (Fifth Study, I and II.)

Lesson XIII.—*The Rise of the Israelite Empire.* The reign of Saul. (Fifth Study, III.)

Lesson XIV.—*The Rise of the Israelite Empire.* The reign of David. (Fifth Study, IV.) Also review Fifth Study.

Lesson XV.—*The Golden Age of Israel.* Reign of Solomon. (Sixth Study, I.)

Lesson XVI.—*The Golden Age of Israel.* General aspect of Israel and dangers of the period. (Sixth Study, II and III.)

Lesson XVII.—*The Empire of Israel.* Review the reigns of Saul, David, and Solomon. (Fifth Study, III, IV, and Sixth Study, I, II, III.)

Lesson XVIII.—*Israel.* Causes and results of division. (Seventh Study, I and II.)

Lesson XIX.—*Israel.* Kingdom of Israel. (Seventh Study, III.)

Lesson XX.—*Israel.* Fate of ten tribes. (Seventh Study, IV.) Also review Seventh Study.

Lesson XXI.—*Judah.* General aspects and duration of the kingdom. (Eighth Study, I and II.)

Lesson XXII.—*Judah.* Periods in its history. (Eighth Study, III.) Also review Seventh and Eighth Studies.

Lesson XXIII.—*The Captivity of Judah.* Captivities of Judah and Israel, and three captivities of Judah. (Ninth Study, I and II.)

Lesson XXIV.—*The Captivity of Judah.* Causes of captivity. (Ninth Study, III.)

Lesson XXV.—*The Captivity of Judah.* Condition of the captives. (Ninth Study, IV.)

Lesson XXVI.—*The Captivity of Judah.* Results of the captivity. (Ninth Study, V.)

Lesson XXVII.—*The Captivity of Judah.* Review of Ninth Study.

Lesson XXVIII.—*The Jewish Province.* Persian. (Tenth Study, I, II.)

Lesson XXIX.—*The Jewish Province.* Greek periods. (Tenth Study, II.)

Lesson XXX.—*The Jewish Province.* Maccabean and Roman periods. (Tenth Study, III, IV.)

Lesson XXXI.—*The Jewish Province.* Preparation for the temple. (Tenth Study, V.)

Lesson XXXII.—Review of Tenth Study.

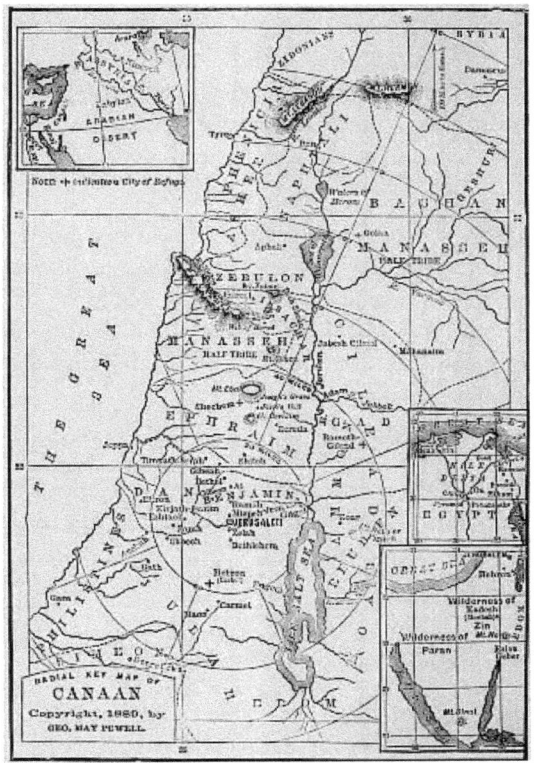

STUDIES IN OLD TESTAMENT HISTORY.

FIRST STUDY.
THE BEGINNINGS OF BIBLE HISTORY.

It is our purpose in this series of studies to trace the progress of events as related in the Bible from the dawn of history down to the opening of the New Testament era. The aim will be not to give a mere catalogue of facts, but rather to show the relation of cause and effect, and to unfold the development of the divine purpose which extends through all the history in the Bible. We recommend the student, first of all, to read the preface to this book.

Turning back to the beginnings of Bible history we notice **six events** between the Deluge and the Exodus. We begin with the Deluge as the starting-point of history. Back of that event is a land of shadows. We have so little knowledge of the world before the flood that its history cannot be written. But since that fact we tread upon firm ground, having both the Bible and secular history to confirm each other.

I. **THE DELUGE.** With regard to this event we note:

1. The **fact** of a general deluge is stated in Scripture (Gen. 7.), and attested by the traditions of nearly all nations. Compare the story of Xisuthros in Berosus; the record in the Chaldean tablets; the Greek myth of Deucalion; the Mexican tradition; and the legends of the North American Indians.[A]

2. The **date** is given in reference Bibles (following Archbishop Ussher) as B. C. 2348. This is probably incorrect. It may have been a thousand years earlier. But as archæologists are not yet agreed, we give Ussher's chronology, here and elsewhere, merely as a convenience in the arrangement, not as accurate.

3. Its **cause** was the wickedness of the human race (Gen. 6. 5-7). Before this event all the population of the world was massed together, forming one vast family and speaking one language. Under these conditions the good were overborne by evil surroundings, and general corruption followed.

4. Its **extent** was undoubtedly not the entire globe, but so much of it as was occupied by the human race (Gen. 7. 23), probably the Euphrates valley. Many Christian scholars, however, hold to the view that the Book of Genesis relates the history of but one family of races, and not all the race;

consequently, that the flood may have been partial, as far as mankind is concerned.

5. Its **purpose** was: 1.) To destroy the evil in the world. 2.) To open a new epoch under better conditions for social, national, and individual life.

II. **THE DISPERSION OF THE RACES.** (B.C. 2247?) 1. Very soon after the deluge a new **instinct**, that **of migration**, took possession of the human family. Hitherto all mankind had lived together; from this time they began to scatter. As a result came tribes, nations, languages, and varieties of civilization. "The confusion of tongues" was not the cause, but the result of this spirit, and was not sudden, but gradual (Gen. 11. 2, 7).

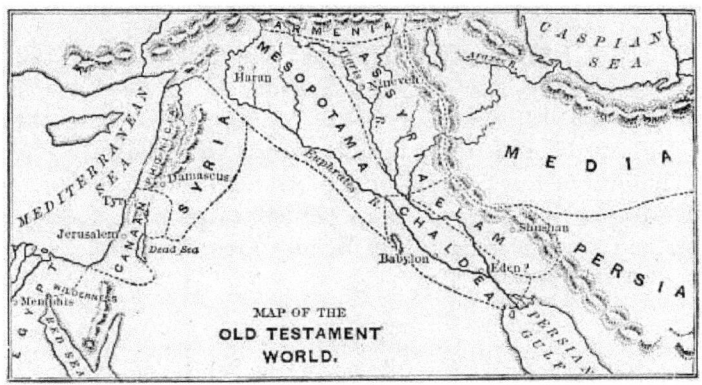

MAP OF THE OLD TESTAMENT WORLD.

2. **Evidences of this migration** are given: 1.) In the Bible (Gen. 9. 19; 11. 8). 2.) The records and traditions of nearly all nations point to it. 3.) Language gives a certain proof; for example, showing that the ancestors of the English, Greeks, Romans, Medes, and Hindus—races now widely dispersed—once slept under the same roof. At an early period streams of migration poured forth from the highlands of Asia in every direction and to great distances.

III. **THE RISE OF THE EMPIRES.** In the Bible world three centers of national life arose, not far apart in time, each of which became a powerful kingdom, and in turn ruled all the Oriental lands. The strifes of these three nations, their rise and fall, constitute the matter of ancient Oriental history, which is closely connected with that of the Bible. These three centers were Egypt (called in the Bible Mizraim, Gen. 10. 6, 13), of which the capital was Memphis; Chaldea, of which the capital was Babel or Babylon (Gen. 10. 10; 11. 2-9); and Assyria, of which the capital was Nineveh (Gen. 10. 11). We might add to these the Canaanite or Phenician city of Sidon (Gen. 10. 15, 19), and its daughter Tyre, the great commercial centers of the ancient world, whose empire was not the land, but the sea. Note that all of these early kingdoms were established by the Hamitic race.

IV. **THE MIGRATION OF ABRAHAM.** (B. C. 1921?) No other journey in history has the *importance* of that transfer of the little clan of Abraham from the plain of Shinar to the mountains of Palestine in view of its results to the world. Compare with it the voyage of the *Mayflower*. Its causes were: 1. Probably the migratory instinct of the age, for it was the epoch of tribal movements. 2. The political cause may have been the desire for liberty from the rule of the Accadian dynasty that had become dominant in Chaldea. 3. But the deepest motive was religious, a purpose to escape from the idolatrous influences of Chaldea, and to find a home for the worship of God in what was then "the new West," where population was thin. It was by the call of God that Abraham set forth on his journey (Gen. 12. 1-3).

V. **THE JOURNEYS OF THE PATRIARCHS.** (B. C. 1921-1706?) For two centuries the little clan of Abraham's family lived in Palestine as strangers, pitching their tents in various localities, wherever pasturage was abundant, for at this time they were shepherds and herdsmen (Gen. 13. 2; 46. 34). Their home was generally in the southern part of the country, west of the Dead Sea, and their relations with the Amorites, Canaanites, and Philistines on the soil were generally friendly (Gen. 20. 14; 26. 26-31).

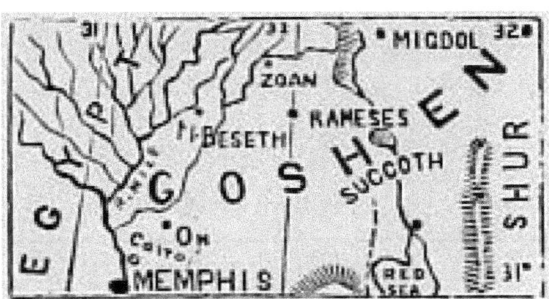

VI. **THE SOJOURN IN EGYPT.** (B. C. 1706-1491?) After three generations the branch of Abraham's family belonging to his grandson Jacob or Israel removed to Egypt (Deut. 26. 5), where they remained either two hundred or four hundred years, according to different opinions.[B] This stay in Egypt is always called "the sojourn." The event which led directly to the descent into Egypt was the selling of Joseph (Gen. 37. 28). But we can trace a providential purpose in the transfer. Its objects were:

- 13 -

1. **Preservation.** The frequent famines in Palestine (Gen. 12. 10; 26. 1;42. 1-3) showed that as shepherds the Israelites could not be supported in the land. On the fertile soil of Egypt, with three crops each year, they would find food in abundance.

2. **Growth.** At the end of the stay in Canaan the Israelites counted only seventy souls (Gen. 46. 27); but at the close of the sojourn in Egypt they had increased to nearly two millions (Exod. 12. 37; Num. 1. 45, 46). The hot climate and cheap food of Egypt has always caused an abundant population. In Egypt Israel grew from a family to a nation.

3. **Isolation.** There was great danger to the morals and religion of the Israelites in the land of Canaan. Abraham had sent to his own relatives at Haran for a wife for Isaac (Gen. 24. 3, 4) in order to keep both the race and the faith pure. One of Isaac's sons married Canaanite wives, and as a result his descendants, the Edomites, lost the faith and became idolaters (Gen. 26. 34, 35). Jacob sought his wives among his own relatives (Gen. 28. 1, 2). We note a dangerous tendency in Jacob's family to ally themselves with the Canaanites (Gen. 34. 8-10; 38. 1, 2). If they had stayed in Canaan the chosen family would have become lost among the heathen. But in Egypt they lived apart, and were kept by the caste system from union with the people (Gen. 46. 34; 43. 32). It was a necessary element in the divine plan that Israel should dwell apart from other nations (Num. 23. 9).

4. **Civilization.** The Egyptians were far in advance of all other nations of that age in intelligence, in the organization of society, and in government. Though the Israelites lived apart from them, they were among them, and learned much of their knowledge. Whatever may have been their condition at the beginning of the sojourn, at the end of it they had a written language (Exod. 24. 7), a system of worship (Exod. 19. 22; 33. 7), and a leader who had received the highest culture of his age (Acts 7. 22). As one result of the sojourn the Israelites were transformed from shepherds and herdsmen to tillers of the soil—a higher manner of living.

Blackboard Outline.

Six Ev. I. Del. 1. Fac. Scrip. Trad. 2. Dat. 2348? 3. Cau. Wick. rac. 4. Ext. par. 5. Pur. 1.) Des. ev. 2.) New ep.
II. Disp. Rac. 1. Inst. mig. 2. Evid. Bib. Trad. Lang.
III. Rise Emp. 1. Eg. 2. Chal. 3. Ass. 4. Sid. and Tyr.
IV. Mig. Abr. Causes. 1. Mig. inst. 2. Pol. cau. 3. Rel. mot.
V. Jour. Patr. Str. in Pal. Shep. Hom. Relat.
VI. Soj. in Eg. Obj. 1. Pres. 2. Gro. 3. Isol. 4. Civ.

QUESTIONS FOR REVIEW.

What is the purpose in this series of studies?
At what point does history begin?
Name the six great events in early Bible history.
How is the fact of a deluge attested?
What date is commonly given to this event?
What was the moral cause of the flood?
What was its extent?
What was its purpose in the plan of God?
What new spirit took possession of men soon after the flood?
To what results did this lead?
What was the relation of this fact to the confusion of tongues?
What evidences of these migrations are found?
What were the three great centers of national life in the Oriental world?
What city became the center of commercial life?
To what race did the earliest empires belong?
What was the most important journey, in its results, in all history?
What three causes are given for this migration?
What was especially the religious motive of this journey?
How long did Abraham's descendants remain in Palestine?
In what part of the country did they live?
What were their relations with the native peoples in Palestine?
What is meant by "the sojourn?"
What was its immediate cause?
What four providential results came to Israel through this sojourn?
How long was the time of the sojourn?
How were the Israelites protected from corruption through this sojourn?
What was the effect of the sojourn upon their civilization?

Subjects for Special Papers.

THE PYRAMIDS.
THE CITY OF BABYLON.
THE GREAT RACES.
TRADITIONS OF THE DELUGE.
THE CHARACTER OF ABRAHAM.
EGYPT IN THE TIME OF JOSEPH.

FOOTNOTES:

[A] See Geikie's *Hours with the Bible*, vol. 1, chap. xiii; *Bible Commentary*, note at the end of Gen. 8.

[B] From the fact that in several genealogies four generations are given to the sojourn in Egypt, the shorter period, from 1706 to 1491, has been generally assumed. But it is almost impossible that seventy people could become two million in four generations by natural increase alone. Moreover, the genealogy of Joshua (1 Chron. 7. 22-27) gives either ten or eleven generations to this period. It is probable that the other tables name only sufficient links to show the line, and omit many of the generations. This was frequently the case with Jewish records. (See the genealogy of Jesus Christ in Matt. 1, where several names are omitted.) We conclude that the sojourn began about 1900 B. C., and the call of Abraham was about 2100 B. C., or earlier; but we give in the text the usual chronology.

SECOND STUDY.
THE WANDERING IN THE WILDERNESS.

I. Let us notice briefly the **EVENTS LEADING TO THE WANDERING.**

1. **The Oppression of the Israelites.** (B. C. 1635.) (Exod. 1. 8-13.) This was an important link in the chain of events. If the Israelites had been prosperous and happy in Egypt they would have remained there, and the destiny of the chosen people would have been forgotten. Therefore, when Egypt had given to Israel all that it could, the wrath of man was made to praise God; and by suffering the Israelites were made willing to leave the land of their sojourn and seek the land of promise. The nest was stirred up, and the young eaglet was compelled to fly (Deut. 32. 11, 12).

2. **The Training of Moses.** (Born B. C. 1571.) There was another element of preparation. No common man could have wrought the great work of liberation, of legislation, and of training which Israel needed. Notice, 1.) Moses was an *Israelite in birth*, of the consecrated tribe of Levi (Exod. 2. 1, 2). 2.) But he was *educated in the palace*, and in the highest culture, as a prince in Egypt (Exod. 2. 10). If he had been doomed to a slave's life he could never have accomplished his mission. 3.) At full age Moses made *choice of his people*, because they were the people of God (Heb. 11. 24-26). 4.) Then came the *training of forty years* in the desert, giving him knowledge of the land, experience of hardships, and maturity of thought. 5.) Lastly, there was the *call of God* (Exod. 3. 2), with its revelation of God's name and power, imparting strength for his work.

3. **The Ten Plagues.** There was a special significance in these plagues, for each was a blow at some form of idol-worship among the Egyptians. They were: 1.) The river turned to blood (Exod. 7. 20, 21). 2.) Frogs (Exod. 8. 6). 3.) Lice (Exod. 8. 17). 4.) Flies, probably including beetles and other winged pests (Exod. 8. 24). 5.) Murrain, or pestilence among domestic animals (Exod. 9. 3, 4). 6.) Boils (Exod. 9. 10). 7.) Hail (Exod. 9. 23). 8.) Locusts (Exod. 10. 14, 15). 9.) Darkness (Exod. 10. 22, 23). 10.) Death of the first-born (Exod. 12. 29).

4. **The Passover.** (Exod. 12. 21-28.) This service represented three ideas. 1.) It was the spring-tide festival. 2.) It commemorated the sudden departure from Egypt, when there was not even time to "raise the bread" before leaving (Exod. 12. 34-39). 3.) It was an impressive prophecy of Christ, the slain Lamb of God (Exod. 12. 21, 22).

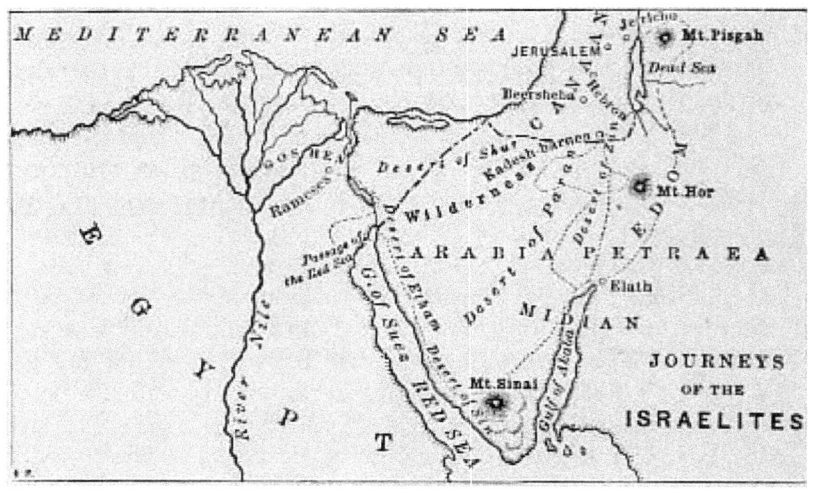

5. **The Exodus.** (B. C. 1491.) (Exod. 12. 40, 41.) The word means "going out." This was the birthday of a nation, the hour when the Israelites rose from being merely a mass of men to become a people.

II. **THE WILDERNESS OF THE WANDERING.** Let the student note carefully upon a good map the following locations, and then draw a map containing them:

1. Draw the coast-lines and note **three Seas**. 1.) The "great sea," or *Mediterranean* (Josh. 1. 4). 2.) The *Red Sea* (Exod. 13. 18), (Gulfs of Suez and Akaba). 3.) The *Dead Sea*.

2. Draw the mountain ranges, and note **five Deserts**. 1.) The *Desert of Shur* (Exod. 15. 22), between Goshen and Canaan. 2.) The *Desert of Paran*, in the center of the Sinaitic triangle (Num. 10. 12). This is the wilderness in which thirty-eight of the forty years were passed (Deut. 1. 19). 3.) The *Desert of E'ham* (Num. 33. 8), on the shore of the Gulf of Suez. 4.) The *Desert of Sin*, near Mount Sinai (Exod. 16. 1). 5.) The *Desert of Zin*, the desolate valley between the Gulf of Akaba and the Dead Sea, now called the Arabah (Num. 13. 21).

3. Locate also the **five Lands** of this region. 1.) *Goshen*, the land of the sojourn (Exod. 9. 26). 2.) *Midian*, the land of Moses's shepherd life (Exod. 2. 15), on both sides of the Gulf of Akaba. 3.) *Edom*, the land of Esau's descendants, south of the Dead Sea (Num. 21. 4). 4.) *Moab*, the land of Lot's descendants, east of the Dead Sea (Num. 21. 13). 5.) *Canaan*, the land of promise (Gen. 12. 7).

4. Fix also the location of **three Mountains**. 1.) *Mount Sinai*, where the law was given (Exod. 19. 20). 2.) *Mount Hor*, where Aaron died (Num. 20. 23-28). 3.) *Mount Nebo* (Pisgah), where Moses died (Deut. 34. 1).

5. Notice also **seven Places**, some of which are clearly, others not so definitely, identified. 1.) *Rameses*, the starting-point of the Israelites (Exod. 12. 37). 2.) *Baal-zephon*, the place of crossing the Red Sea (Exod. 14. 2). 3.) *Marah*, where the bitter waters were sweetened (Exod. 15. 22-25). 4.) *Elim*, the place of rest (Exod. 15. 27). 5.) *Rephidim*, the place of the first battle, near Mount Sinai (Exod. 17. 8-16). 6.) *Kadesh-barnea*,[C] whence the spies were sent forth (Num. 13. 26). 7.) *Jahaz*, in the land of Moab, south of the brook Arnon, the place of a victory over the Amorites (Num. 21. 23, 24).

III. **THE JOURNEYS OF THE WANDERING.** These, with the **EVENTS** connected with them, may be arranged in order as follows:

1. From Rameses to the Red Sea (Exod. 12. 37; 14. 9). With this note: 1.) *The crossing of the Red Sea.*

2. From the Red Sea to Mount Sinai. Events: 2.) *The Waters of Marah.* 3.) *The repulse of the Amalekites.* 4.) *The giving of the law.* 5.) *The worship of the golden calf.* At Mount Sinai the camp was kept for nearly a year, and the organization of the people was effected.

3. From Mount Sinai to Kadesh-barnea (B. C. 1490). At the latter place occurred, 6.) *The sending out of the spies* (Num. 13. 1-26). 7.) *The defeat at Hormah* (Num. 14. 40-45). It was the purpose of Moses to lead the people at once from Kadesh up to Canaan. But their fear of the Canaanite and Amorite inhabitants made them weak; they were defeated and driven back into the desert of Paran, where they wandered thirty-eight years, until the generation of slavish souls should die off, and a new Israel, the young people, trained in the spirit of Moses and Aaron, and fitted for conquest, should arise in their places.

4. From Kadesh-barnea through the desert of Paran and return. This was the long wandering of thirty-eight years. We trace the route from Kadesh, around the desert of Paran, to Mount Hor, to Ezion-geber at the head of the Gulf of Akaba, and at last to Kadesh once more (Num. 20. 1). There occurred, 8.) *The water from the rock at Kadesh*, and Moses's disobedience (Num. 20. 10-12). 9.) *The repulse of Arad* (Num. 21. 1). It would seem that the Israelites made a second attempt to enter Canaan on the south, and were again defeated, though not so severely as before.

5. From Kadesh-barnea around Edom to the river Jordan. After this second defeat Moses desired to lead the people through the land of the Edomites, and to enter Canaan by crossing the Jordan (Num. 20. 14). But the Edomites refused to permit such an army to pass through their land (Num. 20. 18-21). Hence the Israelites were compelled to go down the desert of Zin, past Edom, as far as the Red Sea, then east of Edom, a very long and toilsome journey (Num. 21. 4). Note with this journey: 10.) *The brazen serpent* (Num. 21. 6-9; John 3. 14, 15). 11.) *The victory over the Amorites* (Num. 21. 23, 24). This victory gave to the Israelites control of the country from Amon to Jabbok, and was the first campaign of the conquest. The long journey was now ended in the encampment of the Israelites at the foot of Mount Nebo, on the eastern bank of the Jordan, near the head of the Dead Sea. 12.) The last event of the period was *the death of Moses* (Deut. 34. 5-8) (B. C. 1451).

IV. **THE RESULTS OF THE WANDERING.** These forty years of wilderness life made a deep impress upon the Israelite people, and wrought great changes in their character.

1. It gave them certain **Institutions**. From the wilderness they brought their tabernacle and all its rites and services, out of which grew the magnificent ritual of the temple. The Feast of Passover commemorated the

Exodus, the Feast of Pentecost, the giving of the law; the Feast of Tabernacles (during which for a week the people lived in huts and booths), the outdoor life in the desert.

2. Another result was **National Unity**. When the Israelites left Egypt they were twelve unorganized tribes, without a distinct national life. Forty years in the wilderness, meeting adversities together, fighting enemies, marching as one host, made them a nation. They emerged from the wilderness a distinct people, with one hope and aim, with patriotic self-respect, ready to take their place among the nations of the earth.

3. **Individual Liberty.** They had just been set free from the tyranny of the most complete governmental machine on the face of the earth. In Egypt the man was nothing, the state was every thing. The Israelite system was an absolute contrast to the Egyptian. For four centuries after the Exodus the Israelites lived with almost no government, each man doing what was right in his own eyes. They were the freest people on earth, far more so than the Greeks or the Romans during their republican epochs. Moses trained them not to look to the government for their care, but to be a self-reliant people, able to take care of themselves. If they had passed this initial stage of their history surrounded by kingdoms they would have become a kingdom. But they learned their first lessons of national life in the wilderness, untrammeled by environment and under a wise leader, who sought to train up a nation of kings instead of a kingdom.

4. **Military Training.** We trace in the history of those forty years a great advance in military discipline. After crossing the Red Sea Moses did not care to lead them by the direct route to Canaan, lest they should "see war" (Exod. 13. 17, 18). Attacked by the Amalekites soon after the Exodus, the Israelites were almost helpless (Exod. 17. 8-16; Deut. 25. 17-19). A year later they were the easy prey of the Canaanites at Hormah (Num. 14. 40-45). Forty years after they crossed the Jordan and entered Canaan, a drilled and trained host, a conquering army. This discipline and spirit of conquest they gained under Moses and Joshua in the wilderness.

5. **Religious Education.** This was the greatest of all the benefits gained in the wilderness. They were brought back from the idolatries of Egypt to the faith of their fathers. They received God's law, the system of worship, and the ritual which brought them by its services into a knowledge of God. Moreover, their experience of God's care taught them to trust in Jehovah, who had chosen them for his own people. Even though the mass of the people might worship idols, there was always from this time an Israel of the heart that sought and obeyed God.

Blackboard Outline.

I. Eve. le. Wan. 1. Opp. Isr.
2. Tra. Mos. 1.) Bir. 2.) Edu. 3.) Cho. 4.) Tra. 5.) Cal.
3. Ten Pla. 1.) Bl. 2.) Fr. 3.) Li. 4.) Fl. 5.) Mur. 6.) Boi. 7.) Hai. 8.) Loc. 9.) Dar. 10.) Dea. fir. bo.
4. Pass.
5. Exod.

II. Wil. Wan. 1. Seas. 1.) M. S. 2.) R. S. [G, S., G. A.] 3.) D. S.
2. Des. 1.) D. Sh. 2.) D. Par. 3.) D. Eth. 4.) D. Si. 5.) D. Zi.
3. Lan. 1.) Gos. 2.) Mid. 3.) Ed. 4.) Mo. 5.) Can.
4. Mts. 1.) Mt. Sin. 2.) Mt. H. 3.) Mt. Neb.
5. Pla. 1.) Ram. 2.) B.-zep. 3.) Mar. 4.) El. 5.) Rep. 6.) Kad.-bar 7.) Jah.

III. Jour. and Even. Jour. 1. Ram.—R. S., Ev. 1.) Cr. R. S.
Jour. 2. R. S.—Mt. Sin. 2.) Wat. Mar. 3.) Rep. Am. 4.) Giv. L. 5.) Wor. gol. cal.
Jour. 3. Mt. Sin.—Kad.-bar. 6.) Sen. Sp. 7.) Del. Hor.
Jour. 4. Kad.-bar.—Des. Par.—Ret. 8.) Wat. roc. Kad. 9.) Rep. Ar.
Jour. 5. Kad.-bar.—Ed.—Riv. Jor. 10.) Bra. Ser. 11.) Vic. ov. Amo. 12.) Dea. Mos.

IV. Res. Wan. 1. Ins. 2. Nat. Un. 3. Ind. Lib. 4. Mil. Tra. 5. Rel. Ed.

QUESTIONS FOR REVIEW.

Name five events which were preparatory to the wandering.
What made the Israelites willing to leave Egypt?
How was their leader trained for his mission?
What were the ten plagues upon the Egyptians?
What three ideas were connected with the Passover?
What is meant by the Exodus?
What are the three seas of the map illustrating the wandering?
Name five deserts of this region.
In which desert were the most years passed?
What were the two deserts on the shore of the Red Sea?
Where was the desert of Zin?
Which desert was between Egypt and Palestine?
Name and locate five lands of this region.
Which land was nearest to Egypt?

Which land was on the eastern arm of the Red Sea?
Which land lay east of the Dead Sea?
Which land was south of the Dead Sea?
Name three mountains in this region.
What event took place on each of these mountains?
Name two places between Egypt and the Red Sea.
Name three places on the route between the Red Sea, and an event at each place.
What place was south of Canaan and near it?
What events occurred at this place?
What two places were battlefields?
State the route of the first journey.
What was the great event of this journey?
What was the second journey?
What four events are named with this journey?
What was the third journey?
What two events took place with this journey?
What was the longest journey?
Name four places of this journey.
Name two events near its close.
What was the last journey?
What events took place at this time?
Where was the last encampment of the Israelites?
What institutions originated during this period?
What was the political effect of this epoch upon the people?
How did it give them liberty?
What was the influence in military affairs?
What were its results upon the religion of the people?

Subjects for Special Papers.

THE PHARAOH OF THE OPPRESSION.
MOUNT SINAI.
THE GREATNESS OF MOSES.
THE MOSAIC LEGISLATION.
THE SITE OF KADESH-BARNEA.
THE TABERNACLE IN THE WILDERNESS.

FOOTNOTE:

[C] The location of Kadesh-barnea is one of the great questions of the Bible geography. Robinson places it at *'Ain el-Weibeh*, north-west of Petra. Rowlands, and lately Trumbull, locates it at *Ain Gadis*, forty-five miles south of Beersheba. I think the latter is the true place, though the authorities are not agreed.

THIRD STUDY.
THE CONQUEST OF CANAAN.

I. Let us notice the **CANAANITES** before the conquest.

1. They were a **varied people**. There were from seven to ten different nations in Palestine when the Israelites entered it (Exod. 3. 17; Deut. 7. 1). Each tribe, often each city, had its own government. There was no unity of government, no combined action to resist the invasion of Israel. This made the conquest easy. If one king had ruled a united people the result might have been different.

2. These peoples were, however, of **one stock**. They belonged to the Hamite race, and were all descended from the family of Canaan (Gen. 10. 15-19). There was no reason, except the tribal spirit, for their separation into small clans and nationalities.

3. They were **idolatrous** and, as a result, grossly **immoral**. Idolatry is always associated with immorality; for the worship of idols is a deification of sensuality. Baal and Asherah (plural Ashtoreth) were the male and female divinities worshiped by most of these races (Judg. 2. 13).

4. They had been **weakened** before the coming of the Israelites either by war or by pestilence. The allusions in Exod. 23. 28; Deut. 7. 20; and Josh. 7. 12, have been referred to an invasion before that of Israel, or to some plague, which destroyed the native races.

II. **THE CAMPAIGNS OF THE CONQUEST.** These may be divided as follows:

1. **The campaigns east of the Jordan.** (B. C. 1451.) These were during the life-time of Moses, and gained for Israel all the territory between the brook Arnon and Mount Hermon.

1.) The conquest of Gilead was made at the battle of Jahaz, near the brook Arnon (Num. 21. 21-31). In one battle the Israelites gained the land of Gilead from the Arnon to the Hieromax.

2.) The conquest of Bashan was completed at the battle of Edrei, in the mountainous region.

3.) The conquest of Midian (Num. 31. 1-8) was led by the warrior-priest Phinehas, and by smiting the tribes on the east protected the frontier toward the desert. The land won by these three campaigns became the territory of the tribes of Reuben, Gad, and the half-tribe of Manasseh (Deut. 32).

2. **The campaigns west of the Jordan** (B. C. 1451) were led by Joshua, and showed great tactical skill and resistless energy of action. Joshua led his people across the Jordan and established a fortified camp, the center of operations during all his campaigns, at Gilgal (Josh. 4. 19).

1.) The first invasion was of *central Palestine*, beginning with Jericho (Josh. 6), taking Ai on the way (Josh. 8), and ending with Shechem, which apparently fell without resistance (Josh. 8. 30-33). This campaign gave to Israel the center of the land and divided their enemies into two sections.

2.) Next came the campaign against *southern Palestine*. At this time was fought the battle of Beth-horon (Josh. 10. 10), the most momentous in its results in all history, and one over which, if ever, the sun and moon might well stand still (Josh. 10. 12, 13).[D] After this great victory Joshua pursued his enemies and took the towns as far south as Hebron and Debir (Josh. 10. 29-39).

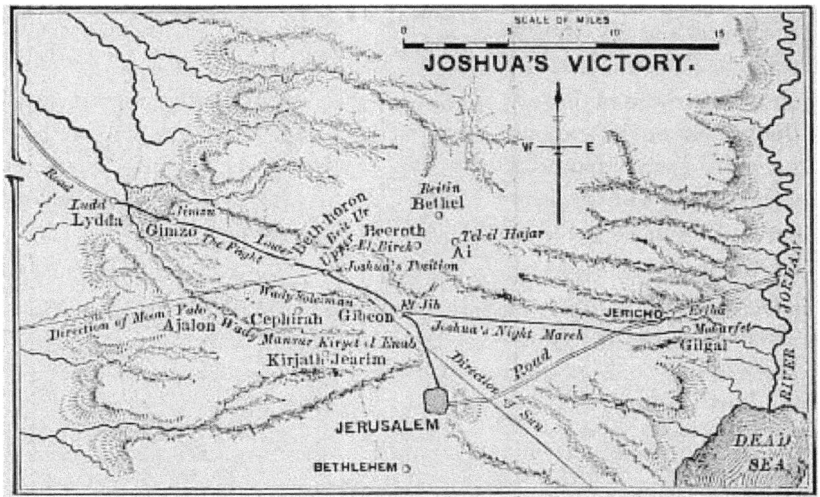

3.) Lastly, Joshua conquered *northern Palestine* (Josh. 11). The battle in this campaign was near Lake Merom (Josh. 11. 7), and, as before, it was followed by the capture of many cities in the north. Thus, in those marches Joshua won all the mountain region of western Palestine.

3. There were certain **supplementary campaigns**, partly in Joshua's time, partly afterward.

1.) Caleb's rapture of Hebron, which had been re-occupied by the Amorites (Josh. 14; Judg. 1. 10-15).

2.) The Judahites' capture of Bezek, an unknown place between Jerusalem and the Philistine plain (Judg. 1. 1-8).

3.) The Danites' capture of Laish, in the extreme north, which afterward bore the name of Dan (Judg. 18).

But, after all these campaigns, a large part of the land was still unsubdued, and the war of the conquest did not end until the days of David, by whom every foe was finally placed under foot.

III. **GENERAL ASPECTS OF ISRAEL AT THE CLOSE OF THE CONQUEST.**

1. With regard to **the native races**. They were not destroyed nor driven away, as had been commanded.[E] They remained as subject people in some places, as the ruling race on the sea-coast and in the Jordan valley. We see their influence, always injurious, throughout all Israel's history (Exod.

23. 31-33; Deut. 7. 1-5); and some think that the present inhabitants of the country belong to the original Canaanite stock.

2. **The Israelites** did not occupy all the country. They possessed most of the mountain region, but none of the sea-coast plain on the Jordan valley. They were like the Swiss in modern times, living among the mountains. Even in the New Testament period the lowlands were occupied mainly by Gentiles.

3. **The landed system** was peculiar. Estates were inalienable. They might be leased, but not sold; and on the year of Jubilee (every fiftieth year) all land reverted to the family originally owning it. Thus every family had its ancestral home, the poor were protected, and riches were kept within bounds.

4. **The government** was a republic of families without an executive head, except when a judge was raised up to meet special needs. Each tribe had its own rulers, but there was no central authority after Joshua (Judg. 21. 25). This had its evils, for it led to national weakness; but it had its benefits: 1.) It kept Israel from becoming a great worldly kingdom like Egypt and Assyria, which would have thwarted the divine purpose. 2.) It promoted individuality and personal energy of character. There would have been no "age of heroes" if Israel had been a kingdom like Egypt.

5. The **religious system** was simple. There was but one altar at Shiloh for all the land and for all the tribes, and the people were required to visit it for the three great feasts (Deut. 12. 11, 14; Josh. 18. 1). This was the religious bond which united the people. If it had been maintained they would have needed no other constitution, and even its partial observance kept the people one nation.

6. The **character** of the people was diverse. Throughout the history we trace the working of two distinct elements. There was the true Israel—the earnest, religious, God-worshiping section, the Israel of Joshua and Gideon and Samuel. Then there was the underlying mass of the people—secular, ignorant, prone to idolatry, the Israel that worshiped Baal and Ashtoreth, and sought alliance with the heathen. One element was the hope of the nation, the other was its bane.

Blackboard Outline.

I. Canaanites. 1. Var. 2. Ham. rac. 3. Idol. 4. Weak.

II. Camp. Conq. 1. Camp. Eas. Jor. 1.) Gil. Jah. 2.) Bash. Ed. 3.) Mid.
2. Camp. Wes. Jor. 1.) Cent. Pal. Jer. Ai. She. 2.) Sou. Pal. Beth-hor. 3.)

Nor. Pal. L. Mer.
3. Supp. Camp.   1.) Cal. cap. Heb.   2.) Jud. cap. Bez.   3.) Dan. cap. Lai.
III. Gen. Asp. Isr. at Clo. Conq.   1. Nat. rac. sub.   2. Isr. in mtn. reg.   3. Land. sys.   4. Gov. rep. fam.   5. Rel. sys.   6. Char. peo.

QUESTIONS FOR REVIEW.

What was the political system of the Canaanites before the conquest?
How did this condition affect the result of the war?
To what race did the Canaanite tribes belong?
What was their religion?
What was the effect of their worship on their character?
What had taken place shortly before the coming of the Israelites?
What campaigns of conquest were made before the death of Moses?
What battles were fought in these campaigns?
What tribes took possession of this territory?
On which side of the Jordan were Joshua's campaigns?
What traits as a military leader did he show?
What places were captured on the first of Joshua's campaigns?
What was the effect of this campaign on the enemies?
Against what section was Joshua's second campaign?
Where was the great battle fought?
What is said to have taken place at this battle?
What cities were captured at this time?
Where was the third campaign of Joshua directed?
Where was the battle fought in this campaign?
What were the three supplementary campaigns?
What city was conquered by Caleb?
What city was occupied by the tribe of Dan?
What king, long after Joshua, completed the conquest of Canaan?
What was the condition of the native races after the conquest?
What was the result of their continuance in the land?
What portion of the country was occupied by the Israelites?
What modern analogy is given to them?
What was the system of land-tenure among the Israelites?
What were some of its benefits?
What was the form of government?
Wherein was this system defective?
What were its excellences?
What was the religious system of the Israelites?
What was the effect of this system?
What was the religious character of the people?
What was the condition of the mass of the Israelites?

Subjects for Special Papers.

JOSHUA AS A GENERAL.
BETH-HORON AS ONE OF THE WORLD'S GREATEST BATTLES.
THE MORAL ASPECTS OF THE DESTRUCTION OF THE CANAANITES.
THE RIVER JORDAN.
THE HISTORY OF JERICHO.

FOOTNOTES:

[D] The account of the sun and moon standing still is an extract from an ancient poem, and is so printed in the Revised Version. The subject is discussed in Geikie's *Hours With the Bible*, foot-note with chapter xiii.

[E] With regard to the destruction of the Canaanites: 1. Such destruction was the almost universal custom of the ancient world. 2. It was deserved by the Canaanites, who were among the most wicked of ancient peoples. 3. It was necessary, if Israel was to be kept from the corruption of their morals, and upon Israel's character depended the world in after ages. 4. As a result of failing to extirpate the Canaanites a vastly greater number of the Israelites were destroyed during the succeeding centuries.

FOURTH STUDY.
THE AGE OF THE HEROES.

From the death of Joshua (about B. C. 1426) to the coronation of Saul (B. C. 1095) the twelve tribes of Israel were without a central government, except as from time to time men of ability rose up among them. It was not as some have supposed, "an age of anarchy," for anarchy is confusion; and during most of the three hundred and thirty years there were peace and order in Israel. It was rather an age of heroes, for its rulers were neither hereditary nor elective, but men called forth by the needs of the hour and their own qualities of leadership.

I. **THE CONDITION OF ISRAEL DURING THIS PERIOD.** This was partly favorable, and partly unfavorable. The favorable elements were:

1. **The mountain location** of Israel. The tribes were perched like Switzerland in the Alps. There was a desert on the south and on the east, while on the west lay the plain by the sea, the great route of travel between Egypt and the Euphrates. Great armies passed and repassed over this plain, and great battles were fought by Egyptians, Hittites, and Assyrians, while Israel on her mountain peaks was unmolested. This mountain home left Israel generally unnoticed, and, when attacked, almost inaccessible.

2. **The racial unity** of Israel. The two finest races of the world, the Greek and the Israelite, were both of pure blood. The Israelites were one in origin, in language, in traditions, in aspirations. This national unity often brought the tribes together in times of distress; though not always when their union was needed.

3. **The religious institutions.** In Greece every town had its own god and its own religion; hence the many parties and petty nationalities. But in Israel there was in theory but one altar, one house of God, one system of worship, with its annual pilgrimage to the religious capital (1 Sam. 1. 3). Just to the measure in which these institutions were observed, Israel was strong against all foes, and as they were neglected the land became the prey of oppressors (Judg. 2. 7-14; 1. Sam. 7. 3).

But there were also unfavorable elements in the condition of Israel, which threatened its very existence. These were:

1. **The native races.** These were of two kinds: the subject peoples left on the soil, more or less under the domination of the conquerors, and the surrounding nations, Ammon, Moab, Syria, and the Philistines. There was

danger from their enmity, a rebellion of the subject tribes, allied with the enemies around, for the destruction of Israel. And there was far greater danger from their friendship, which would lead to intermarriage, to idolatry, to corruption of morals, and to ruin (Judg. 3. 1-7).

2. **Lack of a central government.** Israel was in the condition of the United States at the close of the Revolution, from 1783 to 1789, a loose confederation with no central authority. There were twelve tribes, but each governed itself. Only under some great chieftain like Gideon or Samuel were all the twelve tribes united. Most of the judges ruled only over their own district of a few adjoining tribes. Often the northern tribes were in peril, but we never read of Judah going to their assistance; and in Judah's wars with the Philistines the northern tribes stood aloof.

3. **Tribal jealousy.** Until the establishment of the American republic the world never saw, for any length of time, a league of states on an equal footing. In Greece the strongest state claimed the *hegemony*, or leadership, and oppressed its allies. In Italy the Romans reduced all their neighbors to subjection. In Europe it now requires an army of more than a million men to maintain the "balance of power." So in Israel there was a constant struggle for the leadership between the two great tribes of Judah and Ephraim. During the period of the judges Ephraim was constantly asserting its right to rule the other tribes (Judg. 8. 1-3; 12. 1-6). We trace this rivalry through all the reign of David; and at last it led to the division of the empire under Rehoboam.

4. **Idolatrous tendencies.** We note constantly "the two Israels"—a spiritual minority and an irreligious, idolatrous mass. For ten centuries the greatest evil of Israelite history was the tendency to the worship of idols. Causes which operated to promote it were: 1.) The natural craving for a visible object of worship, not altogether eradicated from even the Christian heart; for example, Romish images and ritualistic bowing toward the altar. 2.) The association of Israel with idolaters on the soil or as neighbors. 3.) The opportunity which idol-worship gives to gratify lust under the guise of religion. As a result of these forces we find idol-worship the crying sin of the Israelites down to the captivity in Babylon.

II. **THE JUDGES OF ISRAEL.** These were the heroes of that age, the men who in turn led the tribes, freed them from their enemies, and restored them to the service of God.

1. **Their office.** It was not generally to try legal cases between man and man, or between tribe and tribe. It might be regarded as a military dictatorship blended with a religious authority. The judge was a union of the warrior and the religious reformer.

2. **Their appointment**; not by election, nor the votes of the people. The Orientals have never chosen their rulers by suffrage. The judges were men whom the people recognized as called of God to their office (Judg. 2. 16; 3. 9; 6. 11-13).

3. **Their authority** rested not on law, nor on armies, but on the personal elements of integrity and leadership in the men, and on the general belief in their inspiration. They spoke to the people with the authority of a messenger from God. They arose in some hour of great need, and after the immediate danger was over held their power until the end of their lives.

4. **The extent of their rule** was generally local, over a few tribes in one section. Deborah ruled in the north (Judg. 5. 14-18); Jephthah governed the east of the Jordan only (Judg. 11. 29). Often more than one judge was ruling at the same time; probably Samson and Eli were contemporaneous. Gideon and Samuel alone ruled all the twelve tribes.

III. **THE OPPRESSIONS AND DELIVERERS.** During these three centuries the influences already named brought Israel many times under the domination of foreign power. The story was always the same, forsaking God, following idols, subjection, reformation, victory, and temporary prosperity. We notice the seven oppressions. Some of these were undoubtedly contemporaneous.

1. **The Mesopotamian Oppression.** (Judg. 3. 7-11.) Probably this was over the southern portion, and the invaders came by the east and around the Dead Sea, as earlier invaders from the same land had come (Gen. 14. 1-7). The deliverer was Othniel, the first judge, and the only judge of the tribe of Judah.

2. **The Moabite Oppression.** (Judg. 3. 12-30.) Over the eastern and central section, including Ephraim (verse 27); deliverer, Ehud, the second judge; battle fought at the ford of the river Jordan (verse 28).

3. **The Early Philistine Oppression.** (Judg. 3. 31.) Over the south-west, on the frontier of Judah; deliverer, Shamgar.

4. **The Canaanite Oppression.** (Judg. 4.) Over the northern tribes; deliverer, Deborah, the woman judge; battle at Mount Tabor.

5. **The Midianite Oppression.** (Judg. 6. 1-6.) Over the northern center, especially Manasseh-east; the most severe of all; deliverer, Gideon, the greatest of the judges (Judg. 6. 11, 12); battle, on Mount Gilboa (Judg. 7), followed by other victories (Judg. 8).

6. **The Ammonite Oppression.** (Judg. 10. 7-9.) Note an alliance between the Amorites and Philistines, which is suggestive; mainly over the

tribes on the east of Jordan; deliverer, Jephthah[F] (Judg. 11); victory at Aroer (verse 33).

7. **The Philistine Oppression.** (Judg. 13) This was the most protracted of all, for it extended, with intervals of freedom, for a hundred years; embraced all the land, but was most heavily felt south of Mounts Carmel and Gilboa. The liberation was begun by Samson (Judg. 13. 5), but he was led astray by sensual lusts and became a failure. Freedom was later won by Samuel at the battle of Ebenezer (1 Sam. 7. 7-14); but the oppression was renewed in the time of Saul, and became heavier than ever (1 Sam. 13. 17-20). Finally the yoke was broken by David, in a succession of victories, ending with the capture of Gath, the Philistine capital (2 Sam. 5. 17-25; 1 Chron. 18. 1).

Note with each oppression: 1.) The oppressor. 2.) The section oppressed. 3.) The deliverer. 4.) The battlefield.

IV. **THE GENERAL ASPECTS OF THE PERIOD.**

1. It was an age of **individuality**. There was no strong government to oppress the people, to concentrate all the life of the nation at the court, and to repress individuality. Contrast Persia with Greece; Rome under the emperors with Rome as a republic. As men were needed they were raised up, for there was opportunity for character. Hence it was an age of heroes—Othniel, Ehud, Shamgar, Gideon, Jephthah, Samson, Samuel, etc. Free institutions bring strong men to the front.

2. It was an age of **neglect of the law**. During all this period there is no allusion to the law of Moses. Its regulations were ignored, except so far as they belonged to the common law of conscience and right. The laws of Moses were not deliberately disobeyed, but were ignorantly neglected. Even good men, as Gideon and Samuel, built altars and offered sacrifices (Judg. 6. 24; 1 Sam. 7. 9) contrary to the letter of the law of Moses, but obeying its spirit.

3. Nevertheless, it was an age of **progress**. There were alternate advancements and retrogressions; yet we see a people with energy, rising in spite of their hindrances. By degrees government became more settled (1 Sam. 7. 15-17), foreign relations arose (1 Sam. 7. 14; Ruth 1. 1), and the people began to look toward a more stable system (1 Sam. 8. 4-6).

Blackboard Outline.

I. Cond. Isr. *Fav.* 1. Mtn. Loc. 2. Rac. Un. 3. Rel. Ins.
Unfav. 1. Nat. Rac. 2. Lac. cent. gov. 3. Tri. jeal. 4. Idol. ten.

II. Jud. Isr. 1. Off. 2. App. 3. Auth. 4. Ext. ru.

III. Opp. and Deliv.

Opp.	*Sec.*	*Deliv.*	*Batt.-fie.*
1. Mes.	Sou.	Oth.	
2. Moab.	Ea. cen.	Ehu.	For. Jor.
3. Ea. Phil.	So.-wes.	Sham.	
4. Can.	Nor.	Deb.	Mt. Tab.
5. Mid.	Nor. cen.	Gid.	Mt. Gil.
6. Amm.	East.	Jeph.	Aro.
7. Phil.	All.	Sams. Saml.	Eben.
		Dav.	Gath.

IV. Gen. Asp. Per. 1. Ind. 2. Neg. Law. 3. Prog.

QUESTIONS FOR REVIEW.

How long was this period? What were its traits? What were the conditions favorable to Israel during this period? How did their location aid the Israelites? Wherein were the Israelites one people? How did their religious institutions keep them together?

What were the unfavorable and dangerous elements in the condition of Israel? How were they in danger from the native races? What was lacking in the government of Israel? What two tribes were in rivalry? What was the effect of this jealousy? What analogy is found in ancient history? How is the same principle illustrated in modern times? What evil tendency was manifested in Israel through nearly all its history? What causes are assigned for this tendency?

What was the office of a judge in Israel? How were the judges appointed? What was their authority? How widely did their rule extend?

What resulted from these evil tendencies in Israel? How many oppressors were there? Who were the first oppressors? Over what part of the country was the first oppression? Who delivered Israel from it? What was the second oppression? What part of the country suffered from it? Who was the deliverer? Where was the battle fought? What was the third oppression, and where? Who delivered Israel? What was the fourth oppression? Where was it? Who was the deliverer? Where was the victory won? What was the fifth oppression? Over what part of the country was it? Who delivered Israel from it? What was the sixth oppression? Over what part of the land was it? Who delivered from it? What was the last oppression? How did it differ from the others? What three names are associated in the deliverance from its power?

What are the three general aspects of this period?

Subjects for Special Papers.

THE ISRAELITE REPUBLIC.
THE CAREER OF GIDEON.
THE VOW OF JEPHTHAH.
THE FAILURE OF SAMSON.
SHILOH AND THE TABERNACLE.
FAMILY LIFE DURING THE AGE OF THE JUDGES.

FOOTNOTE:

[F] With Jephthah is associated the only instance of human sacrifice offered to Jehovah in all Bible history; and this was by an ignorant freebooter, in a part of the land farthest from the instructions of the tabernacle and the priesthood. When we consider that the practice of human sacrifice was universal in the ancient world, and that not only captives taken in war but also the children of the worshipers were offered (2 Kings 3. 26, 27; Mic. 6. 7), this fact is a remarkable evidence of the elevating power of the Israelite worship.

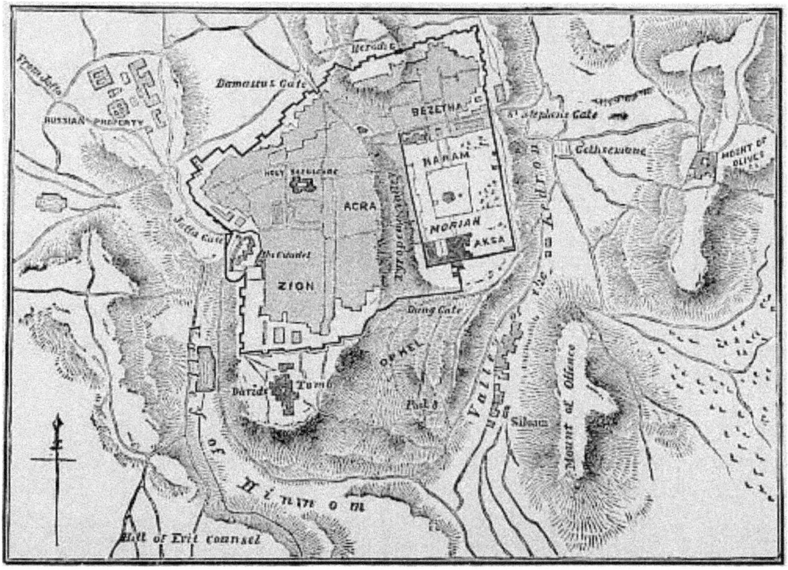

From Jaffa
RUSSIAN PROPERTY
Damascus Gate
Herod's
BEZETHA
St. Stephens Gate
Gethsemane
MOUNT OF OLIVES
HOLY SEPULCHRE
ACRA
HARAM
NORIAH
AKSA
Jaffa Gate
The Citadel
ZION
Dung Gate
OPHEL
David's Tomb
Siloam
Mount of Offence
of Hinnom
Hill of Evil counsel

FIFTH STUDY.
THE RISE OF THE ISRAELITE EMPIRE.

The coronation of Saul (B. C. 1095) marks an epoch in the history of Israel. From that point, for five hundred years, the chosen people were under the rule of kings.

I. **THE CAUSES LEADING TO THE MONARCHY.** The kingdom was not an accidental nor a sudden event. There had been a gradual preparation for it through all the period of the judges.

1. Note the **tendency toward settled government**. In the time of Gideon the people desired him to become a king (Judg. 8. 22, 23). His son attempted to make himself a king, but failed (Judg. 9). We find judges setting up a semi-royal state, and making marriages for their children outside of their tribe (Judg. 12. 9, 13, 14). Judges associating their sons with themselves (Judg. 10. 4; 1 Sam. 8. 1, 2). All these show a monarchical trend in the time.

2. Another cause was the **consolidation of the surrounding nations**. In the days of the conquest there were few kings in the lands neighboring Palestine. We read of "lords" and "elders," but no kings, among the Philistines, the Moabites, the Ammonites, and the Phenicians (Judg. 3. 3; 1 Sam. 5. 8; Num. 22. 7). But a wave of revolution swept over all those lands, as about the same time over Greece; and very soon we find that every nation around Israel had its king (1 Sam. 21. 10; 11. 1; 22. 3; 2 Sam. 5. 11). The movement of Israel toward monarchy was in accordance with this spirit.

3. There was a **danger of invasion**, which impelled the Israelites to seek for a stronger government (1 Sam. 12. 12). They felt themselves weak, while other nations were organized for conquest, and desired a king for leader in war.

4. Then, too, the **rule of Samuel** led the Israelites to desire a better organization of the government. For twenty years they had enjoyed the benefit of a wise, strong, and steady rule. They felt unwilling to risk the dangers of tribal dissension after the death of Samuel, and therefore they sought for a king.

5. But underlying all was the **worldly ambition** of the people. They were not willing to remain the people of God, and work out a peculiar destiny. They wished to be like the nations around, to establish a secular state, to conquer an empire for themselves (1 Sam. 8. 5-20). It was this

worldly spirit, whose results Samuel saw, which made him unwilling to accede to the wish of the Israelites. But the very things against which he warned them (1 Sam. 8. 11-18) were just what they desired.

II. **THE CHARACTER OF THE ISRAELITE KINGDOM.** When men change their plans God changes his. He desired Israel to remain a republic, and not to enter into worldly relations and aims. When, however, the Israelites were determined, God gave them a king (1 Sam. 8. 22); but his rule was not to be like that of the nations around Israel. We ascertain the divine ideal of a kingdom for his chosen people:

1. **It was a theocratic kingdom.** That is, it recognized God as the supreme ruler, and the king as his representative, to rule in accordance with his will, and not by his own right. Only as people and king conformed to this principle could the true aims of the kingdom be accomplished (1 Sam. 12. 13-15). And if the king should deviate from this order, he should lose his throne. Disobedience to the divine will caused the kingdom to pass from the family of Saul to that of David (1 Sam. 13. 13, 14; 15. 26).

2. **It was a constitutional kingdom.** The rights of the people were carefully guaranteed, and there was a written constitution (1 Sam. 10. 25). Nearly all the Oriental countries have always been governed by absolute monarchs; but Israel was an exception to this rule. The people could demand their rights from Rehoboam (1 Kings 12. 3, 4). Ahab could not take away nor even buy Naboth's vineyard against its owner's will (1 Kings 21. 1-3). No doubt the rights of the people were often violated; but the violation was contrary to the spirit of the monarchy.

3. **It was regulated by the prophets.** The order of prophets had a regular standing in the Israelite state. The prophet was a check upon the power of the king, as a representative both of God's will and the people's rights. He spoke not only of his own opinions, but by the authority of God. Notice instances of the boldness of prophets in rebuking kings (1 Sam. 15. 16-23; 2 Sam. 12. 1-7; 1 Kings 13. 1-6; 17. 1; 22. 7-17). The order of prophets was like the House of Commons, between the king and the people.

III. **THE REIGN OF SAUL.** (B. C. 1095-1055.) 1. This may be divided into two parts: 1.) *a period of prosperity*, during which Saul ruled well, and freed Israel from its oppressors on every side (1 Sam. 14. 47, 48); 2.) then a *period of decline*, in which Saul's kingdom seems to be falling in pieces, and only preserved by the prowess and ability of David. After David's exile the Philistines again overran Israel, and Saul's reign ended in defeat and death.

2. We observe that Saul's reign was **a failure**, and left the tribes in worse condition than it found them. 1.) He failed *in uniting the tribes*; for tribal jealousies continued (1 Sam. 10. 27), and at the close of his reign broke out anew in the establishment of rival thrones (2 Sam. 2. 4, 8, 9). 2.) He failed *in making friends*. He alienated Samuel, and with him the order of prophets (1 Sam. 15. 35); he alienated David, the ablest young man of his age, and the rising hope of Israel, and drove him into exile (1 Sam. 21. 10); he alienated the entire order of the priests, and caused many of them to be massacred (1 Sam. 22. 18). 3.) He failed *to advance religion*; left the tabernacle in ruins; left the ark in seclusion; broke up the service; and drove the priests whom he did not murder into exile (1 Sam. 22. 20-23). 4.) He failed *to liberate Israel*; at his death the yoke of the Philistines was more severe than ever before (1 Sam. 31. 1-7). The most charitable view of Saul was that he was insane during the latter years of his life. The cause of his failure was a desire to reign as an absolute monarch, and an unwillingness to submit to the constitution of the realm.

IV. **THE REIGN OF DAVID.** (B. C. 1055-1015.) This was a brilliant period; for it was led by a great man, in nearly every respect the greatest after Moses in Israelite history.

1. Notice the **condition of Israel at his accession**. This will throw into relief the greatness of his character and his achievements.

1.) It was a *subject people*; under Philistine yoke; its warriors slain; many of its cities deserted; David himself probably at first tributary to the King of Gath.

2.) It was a *disorganized people*. The tribes were divided; national unity was lost; and two thrones were set up, one at Hebron, the other at Mahanaim (2 Sam. 2. 4-9).

3.) It was a *people without religion*. The tabernacle was gone; the ark was in neglect; there was no altar and no sacrifice; the priests had been slain.

We can scarcely imagine Israel at a lower ebb than when David was called to the throne.

2. We ascertain **David's achievements**; the results of his reign. 1.) *He united the tribes*. At first crowned king by Judah only, later he was made king over all the tribes, by the desire of all (2 Sam. 5. 1-5). During his reign we find but little trace of the old feud between Ephraim and Judah, though it was not dead, and destined yet to rend the kingdom asunder.

2.) *He subjugated the land*. The conquest of Palestine, left incomplete by Joshua, and delayed for three hundred years, was finished at last by David in the capture of Jebus or Jerusalem (2 Sam. 5. 6, 7), in the overthrow of the Philistines (2 Sam. 5. 17-25), and in the final capture of their capital city (1 Chron. 18. 1). At last Israel was possessor of its own land.

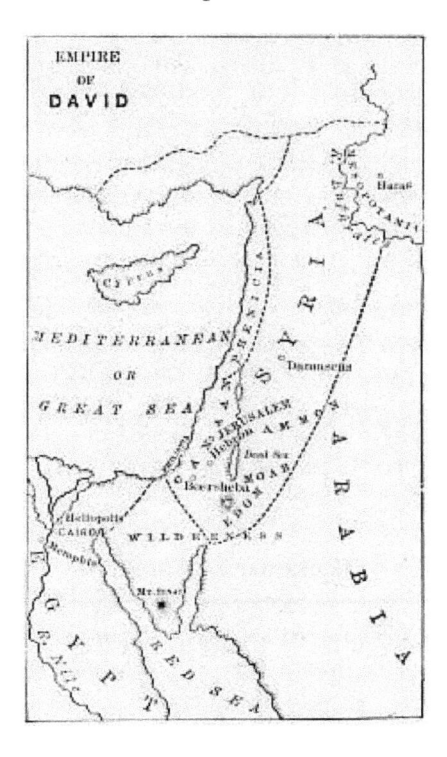

3.) *He organized the government.* He established a capital (2 Sam. 5. 9). He built a palace (2 Sam. 5. 11). Notice that the builders were from Tyre, showing that the Israelites were not advanced in the arts. He established a system of government, with officers in the court and throughout the realm (1 Chron. 27. 25-34). Contrast all this with Saul, who ruled from his tent, like a Bedouin sheik.

4.) *He established an army.* There was a royal body-guard, probably of foreigners, like that of many European kings in modern times (2 Sam. 8. 18; 15. 18). There was a band of heroes, like Arthur's Round Table (2 Sam. 23. 8-39). There was "the host," the available military force, divided into twelve divisions, one on duty each month (1 Chron. 27. 1-15).

5.) *He established religion.* No sooner was David on the throne than he brought the ark out of its hiding-place, and gave it a new home in his capital (1 Chron. 16. 1). The priesthood was organized, and divided into courses for the service of the tabernacle (1 Chron. 23. 27-32; 24. 1-19). He wrote many psalms, and caused others to be written, for the worship of God. Two prophets stood by his throne (1 Chron. 29. 29), and two high-priests stood by the altar (1 Chron. 24. 3). This organization and uplifting of the public worship had a great effect upon the kingdom.

6.) *He conquered all the surrounding nations.* These wars were largely forced upon David by the jealousy of the neighboring kingdoms. In turn his armies conquered and annexed to his dominions the land of the Philistines (1 Chron. 18. 1), Moab (2 Sam. 8. 2), Syria, even to the great river Euphrates (2 Sam. 8. 3-6); Edom (2 Sam. 8. 14), Ammon, and the country east of Palestine (2 Sam. 10. 1-14; 12. 26-31). The empire of David thus extended from the frontier of Egypt to the Euphrates River, fulfilling the promise of Josh 1. 4. It was at least six times the area of the twelve tribes.

7.) We may add that *he reigned as a theocratic king.* He realized more than any other monarch the divine ideal of a ruler, and so was "the man after God's own heart" (1 Sam. 13. 14); if not altogether in personal character, yet in the principles of his government. He respected the rights of his subjects, had a sympathy for all people, obeyed the voice of the prophets, and sought the interests of God's cause.[G]

Blackboard Outline.

I. Cau. lea. Mon. 1. Ten. tow. set. gov. 2. Con. sur. nat. 3. Dan. inv. 4. Ru. Sam. 5. Wor. am. peo.

II. Char. Isr. Kin. 1. Theo. kin. 2. Cons. kin. 3. Reg. by pro.

III. Rei. Sau. 1. Pros. and Dec. 2. Fai. 1.) Un. tri. 2.) Mak. fri. 3.) Adv. rel. 4.) Lib. Isr.

IV. Rei. Dav. 1. Con. Isr. acc. 1.) Sub. 2.) Dis. 3.) Wit. rel. 2. Dav. Achiev. 1.) Uni. tri. 2.) Sub. la. 3.) Org. gov. 4.) Est. ar. 5.) Est. rel. 6.) Conq. surr. nat. 7.) Rei. theo. kin.

QUESTIONS FOR REVIEW.

What event marks an epoch in Israelite history? What were the causes leading to the monarchy? What events in the period of the judges show a tendency toward settled government? What changes in government in the surrounding nations helped to bring on the monarchy in Israel? From what source did external danger lead the Israelites to desire a king? How had Samuel unconsciously helped to prepare the way for a kingdom? What worldly spirit promoted the same result?

What kind of a kingdom did God intend for Israel? What is a theocratic kingdom? Wherein was Israel an exception among Oriental kingdoms? By what institution was the kingdom regulated? Name some instances of prophets rebuking kings.

Into what two parts may Saul's reign be divided? Wherein was Saul a failure? How did he fail in gaining and holding friends?

What was the condition of Israel when David came to the throne? What were the achievements of David? What great incomplete work did David finish? What did he do in the organization of his kingdom? What was the arrangement of his army? What were his services to the cause of religion? What nations did he conquer? What was the extent of his empire? In what spirit did he rule?

Subjects for Special Papers.

HOW THE REPUBLIC BECAME A MONARCHY.
THE EARLY LIFE OF DAVID.
DAVID AS HERO, STATESMAN, AND POET.
DAVID'S TRAINING FOR THE THRONE.
SAMUEL, THE FOUNDER OF THE PROPHETIC ORDER.
THE CAUSES AND RESULTS OF ABSALOM'S REBELLION.

FOOTNOTE:

[G] With regard to David's crimes against Uriah and his wife, note that no other ancient monarch would have hesitated to commit such an act, or would have cared for it afterward; while David submitted to the prophet's rebuke, publicly confessed his sin, and showed every token of a true repentance.

SIXTH STUDY.
THE GOLDEN AGE OF ISRAEL.

The reign of Solomon (B. C. 1015-975) may be regarded as the culminating period in the history of Israel. But, strictly speaking, the latter part of David's reign and only the former part of Solomon's constitute "the golden age of Israel;" for Solomon's later years manifested a decline, which after his death rapidly grew to a fall.

I. **THE REIGN OF SOLOMON.**

1. **His claim to the throne.** He was one of the youngest of David's sons, the second child of Bath-sheba, born during the culmination of David's reign (1 Chron. 22. 7-9). He obtained the throne by the decree of David, by the choice of God, as the one among David's children best fitted to reign (1 Chron. 28. 5, 6). The principle of primogeniture, or the special right of the eldest son, was not fixed in those times.

2. **His accession** was marked by the execution of three men, Adonijah (1 Kings 2. 24, 25), Joab (1 Kings 2. 28-34), and Shimei (1 Kings 2. 36-46). Two of these had conspired against him, and the third was the last survivor of the house of Saul, and a possible rival for the throne. Their death was dictated by policy, and probably by justice. His throne would not be secure while these men lived.

3. **His empire** embraced all the lands from the Red Sea to the Euphrates, and from the Mediterranean to the Syrian desert, except Phenicia, which was isolated by the Lebanon Mountains. 1.) Besides Palestine he ruled over Edom, Moab, Ammon, Syria (here referring to the district having Damascus as its capital), Zobah, and Hamath. 2.) On the Gulf of Akaba, Ezion-geber was his southern port (1 Kings 9. 26); on the Mediterranean, Gaza (Azzah) was his limit; in the extreme north, Tiphsah, by the Euphrates (1 Kings 4. 24); in the desert, Tadmor, afterward Palmyra (1 Kings 9. 18).

4. **His foreign relations** were extensive, for the first and only time in the history of Israel. 1.) His earliest treaty was *with Tyre* (Phenicia), whose king had been his father's friend (1 Kings 5. 1). What this alliance brought to Solomon (1 Kings 5. 6-10; 2 Chron. 2. 3-14). 2.) His relations *with Egypt*; in commerce (1 Kings 10. 28, 29); in marriage, a bold departure from Israelite customs (1 Kings 3. 1). Probably Psalm 45 was written upon this event. 3.) *With Arabia*, the land bordering on the southern end of the Red

Sea (1 Kings 10. 1-10, 14, 15). 4.) *With India*, which is probably referred to in 1 Kings 9. 26-28. 5.) *With Spain*, probably meant in 1 Kings 10. 22.

5. **His buildings.** 1.) Of these the greatest, the most costly, and the most famous was *the temple* (1 Kings 6. 1). With this building notice: (*a*) The courts and open square, with an inner court inside for the priests only (2 Chron 4. 9). (*b*) The porch (2 Chron 3. 4). (*c*) The holy place (2 Chron. 3. 8; 1 Kings 6. 17). (*d*) The holy of holies (1 Kings 6. 19, 20). (*e*) The chambers for the priests (1 Kings 6. 5, 6). 2.) *His own palace*, situated south of the temple precincts, in the district called Ophel. Its name derived from its columned entrance (1 Kings 7. 1, 2). 3.) *His fortified cities* (1 Kings 9. 17-19). 4.) *His aqueducts*, some of which may still be seen (Eccl. 2. 4-6). No King of Israel ever built so many public works as did Solomon.

6. But all was not bright in the reign of Solomon. We must notice also **his sins**, for they wrought great results of evil in the after years. 1.) That which led to all his other sins was *foreign marriages* (1 Kings 11. 1-4). These were the natural and inevitable result of his foreign relations, and were probably effected for political reasons as well as to add to the splendor of his court. 2.) His *toleration of idolatry*, perhaps actual participation in it (1 Kings 11. 5-8). We cannot over-estimate the harm of Solomon's influence in this direction. At once it allied him with the lower and evil elements in the nation, and lost to him the sympathy of all the earnest souls.[H] 3.) Another of Solomon's sins, not named in Scripture, but referred to in many legends of the East, was his *devotion to magical arts*. He appears in Oriental traditions as the great master of forces in the invisible world, engaging in practices forbidden by the law of Moses (Lev. 19. 31; Deut. 18. 10, 11).

II. GENERAL ASPECTS OF ISRAEL IN THE REIGN OF SOLOMON.

1. **It was a period of peace.** For sixty years there were no wars. This gave opportunity for development, for wealth, and for culture.

2. **It was a period of strong government.** The age of individual and tribal energy was ended, and now all the life of the nation was gathered around the throne. All the tribes were held under one strong hand; tribal lines were ignored in the government of the empire (1 Kings 4. 7-19); every department was organized.

3. **It was a period of wide empire.** It was Israel's opportunity for power in the East; for the old Chaldean empire had broken up, the new Assyrian empire had not arisen, and Egypt was passing through a change of rulers and was weak. For one generation Israel held the supremacy in the Oriental world.

4. **It was a period of abundant wealth.** (1 Kings 3. 12, 13; 4. 20; 10. 23, 27.) The sources of this wealth were: 1.) The *conquests* of David, who had plundered many nations and left his accumulated riches to Solomon (1 Chron. 22. 14-16). 2.) The *tribute* of the subject kingdoms, doubtless heavy (1 Kings 10. 25). 3.) *Commerce* with foreign countries, Egypt, Arabia, Tarshish, and Ophir, in ancient times was not carried on by private enterprise, but by the government. The *trade* of the East from Egypt and Tyre passed through Solomon's dominions, enriching the land. 4.) There were also *taxes* laid upon the people (1 Kings 4. 7; 12. 4). 5.) The erection of *public buildings* must have enriched many private citizens and made money plenty.

5. **It was a period of literary activity.** The books written during this epoch were Samuel, Psalms (in part), Proverbs (in part), and perhaps Ecclesiastes and Solomon's Song. Not all the writings of Solomon have been preserved (1 Kings 4. 32, 33).

III. **DANGERS OF THE PERIOD.** There was an Arabian tradition that in Solomon's staff, on which he leaned, there was a worm secretly gnawing it asunder. So there were elements of destruction under all the splendor of Solomon's throne.

1. **The absolute power of the king.** David had maintained the theocratic constitution of the state; Solomon set it aside and ruled with absolute power in all departments. He assumed priestly functions (1 Kings 8. 22, 54, 64); he abolished tribal boundaries in his administration (1 Kings 4. 7-19); he ignored both priests and prophets, and concentrated all rule in his own person.

2. **The formal character of the worship.** There was a magnificent temple and a gorgeous ritual, but none of the warmth and personal devotion which characterized the worship of David. The fervor of the Davidic psalms is wanting in the literature of Solomon's age.

3. **Luxury and corruption of morals.** These are the inevitable results of abundant riches and worldly association. We do not need the warnings in Prov. 2. 16-19; 5. 3-6, etc., to know that a flood of immorality swept over Jerusalem and Israel.

4. **The burden of taxation.** With a splendid court, an immense harem, and a wealthy nobility came high prices and high taxes; the rich growing richer rapidly, the poor becoming poorer. The events of the next reign show how heavy and unendurable these burdens grew.

5. **Heathen customs.** With the foreign peoples came the toleration of idolatry, its encouragement, and all the abominations connected with it.

Jeroboam could not have established his new religion (1 Kings 12. 28) if Solomon had not already patronized idol-worship.

6. Underlying all was the old **tribal jealousy** of Ephraim and Judah, fostered by an able leader (1 Kings 11. 26), ready to break out in due time, and to destroy the empire.

After all, it is uncertain whether the reign of Solomon was a golden or only a gilded age.

Blackboard Outline.

I. Rei. Sol. 1. Cl. thr. 2. Acc. 3. Emp. [Lands. Cities] 4. For. rel. 1.) Ty. 2.) Eg. 3.) Ar. 4.) Ind. 5.) Sp. 5. Buil. 1.) Tem. 2.) Pal. 3.) For. cit. 4.) Aque. 6. Sins 1.) For. mar. 2.) Tol. idol. 3.) Mag.

II. Gen. Asp. Isr. 1. Pea. 2. Str. gov. 3. Abun. weal. 1.) Conq. 2.) Trib. 3.) Com. 4.) Tax. 5). Pub. build. 5. Lit. art.

III. Dan. Per. 1. Abs. pow. 2. For. wor. 3. Lux. cor. mor. 4. Bur. tax. 5. Hea. cus. 6. Tri. jeal.

QUESTIONS FOR REVIEW.

What is meant by the Golden Age of Israel?
Who was Solomon?
How did Solomon obtain the throne?
What events marked his accession?
What lands were included in his empire?
What were the frontier cities of the empire?
With what foreign countries did Solomon have relations?
What resulted from his alliance with Tyre?
What innovation came from Egypt?
Who visited Solomon from Arabia?
What were the early names of Spain and India?
What four classes of buildings were erected by Solomon?
What were the different parts of his temple?
What was the name given to Solomon's palace?
Name some of the cities which he built and fortified.
What other public works did he build?
What three kinds of sin did Solomon commit?
What was his motive in seeking foreign marriages?

Name five general aspects of Israel in Solomon's reign.
What were the benefits of the peace at that time?
What was the characteristic of Solomon's administration?
What opportunity did the age give to a great empire for Israel?
What were the sources of the wealth in Solomon's age?
How was it a period of literary activity?
What ancient legend illustrates the dangers of Solomon's age?
What were some of these dangers?
Wherein did Solomon set aside the Israelite constitution?
What was the defect in the religion of Solomon's time?
What evils resulted from the wealth of that time?
What caused heavy taxation?
What heathen customs were introduced?
What showed that tribal jealousy was still existing?

Subjects for Special Papers.

THE CHARACTER OF SOLOMON.
WAS AN EMPIRE FOR ISRAEL DESIRABLE?
THE WRITINGS OF SOLOMON.
TARSHISH AND OPHIR.
THE TEMPLE OF SOLOMON.
SOLOMON IN ORIENTAL LEGENDS.

FOOTNOTE:

[H] Notice that while the prophets had been friendly to David, they were strongly opposed to Solomon, and gave aid to his enemy Jeroboam (1 Kings 11. 29-39).

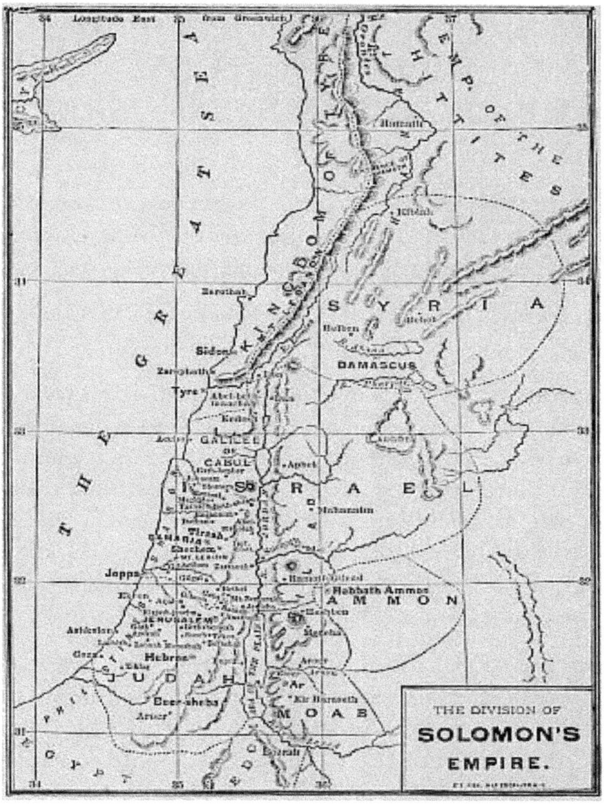
THE DIVISION OF
SOLOMON'S
EMPIRE.
Longitude East
from Greenwich
S Y R I A
DAMASCUS
Sidon
Tyre
GALILEE
CABUL
I S R A E L
Tirzah
Shechem
Joppa
Rabbath Ammon
A M M O N
JERUSALEM
Hebron
J U D A H
Beer-sheba
Ar
M O A B

SEVENTH STUDY.
THE RIVAL THRONES.—ISRAEL.

The splendors of Solomon's reign passed away even more suddenly than they arose. In less than a year after his death his empire was broken up, and two quarreling principalities were all that was left of Israel.

I. Let us ascertain the **CAUSES OF THE DIVISION OF ISRAEL**. These were:

1. **The oppressive government of Solomon.** (1 Kings 12. 3, 4.) How far the complaints of the people were just, and to what degree they were the pretexts of an ambitious demagogue, we have no means of knowing. But it is evident that the government of Solomon, with its court, its palaces, its buildings, and its splendor, must have borne heavily upon the people. Probably, also, the luxury of living among the upper classes, so suddenly introduced, led to financial crises and stringency of money, for which the government was held responsible by the discontented people.

2. **The opposition of the prophets.** (1 Kings 11. 11-13, 29-33.) It is a suggestive fact that the prophets were opposed to Solomon and friendly to Jeroboam. Their reason was a strong resentment to the foreign alliances, foreign customs, and especially to the foreign idolatries which Solomon introduced.

3. **Foreign intrigues**, especially in Egypt. The old kingdoms were not friendly to this Israelite empire, which loomed up so suddenly, and threatened to conquer all the East. Solomon's attempt to win the favor of Egypt by a royal marriage (1 Kings 3. 1) was a failure, for two enemies of Solomon, driven out of his dominions, found refuge in Egypt, were admitted to the court, married relatives of the king, and stirred up conspiracies against Solomon's throne (1 Kings 11. 14-22, 40). Another center of conspiracy was Damascus, where Rezon kept up a semi-independent relation to Solomon's empire (1 Kings 11. 23-25).

4. **Tribal jealousy**; the old sore broken out again. Notice that Jeroboam belonged to the haughty tribe of Ephraim (1 Kings 11. 26), always envious of Judah, and restless under the throne of David. The kingdom of the ten tribes was established mainly through the influence of this tribe.

5. **The ambition of Jeroboam** was another force in the disruption. It was unfortunate for Solomon's kingdom that the ablest young man of that time in Israel, a wily political leader and an unscrupulous partisan, belonged to the tribe of Ephraim, and from his environment was an enemy of the

then existing government. The fact that he was sent for from Egypt to the assembly at Shechem showed collusion and preparation of the scheme (1 Kings 12. 2, 3).

6. But even all these causes might have been insufficient but for **the folly of Rehoboam** (1 Kings 12. 13, 14). If David had been on the throne that day an empire might have been saved. But Rehoboam, brought up in the purple, was without sympathy with the people, tried to act the part of a tyrant, and lost his ancestral realm (1 Kings 12. 16).

II. **THE RESULTS OF THE DIVISION.** These were partly political, partly religious, and were neither of unmixed good nor unmixed evil.

1. The **political results** were: 1.) The entire *disruption* of Solomon's empire. Five kingdoms took the place of one; Syria on the north, Israel in the center, Judah west of the Dead Sea, Moab east of the Dead Sea, and Edom on the extreme south. Moab was nominally subject to Israel, and Edom to Judah; but only strong kings, like Ahab in Israel and Jehoshaphat in Judah, could exact the tribute (2 Kings 3. 4; 1 Kings 22. 47). 2.) With the loss of empire came *rivalry*, and consequent *weakness*. For fifty years Israel and Judah were at war, and spent their strength in civil strife, while Syria was growing powerful, and afar in the north-east Assyria was threatening. 3.) As a natural result came at last *foreign domination*. Both Israel and Judah fell under the power of other nations, and were swept into captivity as the final result of the disruption wrought by Jeroboam.

2. **The religious results** of the division were more favorable. They were: 1.) *Preservation of the true religion.* A great empire would inevitably have been the spiritual ruin of Israel, for it must have been worldly, secular, and, in the end, idolatrous. The disruption broke off relation with the world, put an end to schemes of secular empire, and placed Israel and Judah once more alone among their mountains. In this sense the event was from the Lord, who had higher and more enduring purposes than an earthly empire (1 Kings 12. 15-24). 2.) *Protection of the true religion.* Israel on the north stood as a "buffer," warding off the world from Judah on the south. It was neither wholly idolatrous nor wholly religious, but was a debatable land for centuries. It fell at last, but it saved Judah; and in Judah was the unconscious hope of the world. 3.) *Concentration of the true religion.* The departure of Israel from the true faith led to the gathering of the priests, Levites and worshiping element of the people in Judah (2 Chron. 11. 13-16). Thus the Jewish kingdom was far more devoted to Jehovah than it might otherwise have been.

III. **THE KINGDOM OF ISRAEL.** From the division the name *Israel* was applied to the northern kingdom and *Judah* to the southern. We notice the general aspects of Israel during its history, from B. C. 975 to 721.

1. **Its extent.** It embraced all the territory of the twelve tribes except Judah and a part of Benjamin (1 Kings 12. 19-21), held a nominal supremacy over Moab east of the Dead Sea, and embraced about 9,375 square miles, while Judah included only 3,435. Israel was about equal in area to Massachusetts and Rhode Island together.

2. **Its capital** was at first *Shechem*, in the center of the land (1 Kings 12. 25); then, during several reigns, at *Tirzah* (1 Kings 15. 33; 16. 23); then at *Samaria* (1 Kings 16. 24), where it remained until the end of the kingdom. That city after a time gave its name to the kingdom (1 Kings 21. 1), and after the fall of the kingdom to the province in the center of Palestine (John 4. 3, 4).

3. **Its religion.** 1.) Very soon after the institution of the new kingdom Jeroboam established a national religion, the *worship of the calves* (1 Kings 12. 26-33). This was not a new form of worship, but had been maintained in Israel ever since the Exodus (Exod. 32. 1-4). In character it was a modified idolatry, half-way between the pure religion and the abominations of the heathen. 2.) Ahab and his house introduced the Phenician *worship of Baal*, an idolatry of the most abominable and immoral sort (1 Kings 16. 30-33), but it never gained control in Israel, and was doubtless one cause of the revolution which placed another family on the throne. 3.) Through the history of Israel there remained a remnant of *worshipers of Jehovah*, who were watched over by a noble array of prophets, and though often persecuted remained faithful (1 Kings 19. 14, 18).

4. **Its rulers.** During two hundred and fifty years Israel was governed by nineteen kings, with intervals of anarchy. Five houses in turn held sway, each established by a usurper, generally a soldier, and each dynasty ending in a murder.

1.) *The House of Jeroboam* (B. C. 974 to 953), with two kings, followed by a general massacre of Jeroboam's family (1 Kings 15. 29, 30).

2.) *The House of Baasha* (B. C. 953-929), two kings, followed by a civil war (1 Kings 16. 16-22).

3.) *The House of Omri* (B. C. 929-884), four kings, of whom Omri and Ahab were the most powerful. This was the age of the prophet Elijah and the great struggle between the worship of Jehovah and of Baal (1 Kings 18. 4-21).

4.) *The House of Jehu* (B. C. 884-772), five kings, under whom were great changes of fortune. The reign of Jehoahaz saw Israel reduced to a mere province of Syria (2 Kings 13. 1-9). His son Joash threw off the Syrian yoke, and *his* son, Jeroboam II., raised Israel almost to its condition of empire in the days of Solomon (2 Kings 14. 23-29). His reign is called "the Indian summer of Israel."

5.) *The House of Menahem* (B. C. 772-759), two reigns. Israel had by this time fallen under the power of Assyria, now dominant over the East, and its history is the story of kings rising and falling in rapid succession, with long intervals of anarchy. From the fall of this dynasty there was only the semblance of a state until the final destruction of Samaria, B. C. 721.

5. **Its foreign relations.** During the period of the Israelite kingdom we see lands struggling for the dominion of the East. The history of Israel is interwoven with that of Syria and Assyria, which may now be read from the monuments.

1.) There was a *Period of Division* (B. C. 975-929). During the reign of the houses of Jeroboam and Baasha there were constant wars between Israel, Syria, and Judah; and as a result all were kept weak, and "a balance of power" was maintained.

2.) Then followed a *Period of Alliance* (B. C. 929-884)—that is, between Israel and Judah, during the sway of the House of Omri. The two lands were in friendly relations, and the two thrones were connected by marriages. As a result both Israel and Judah were strong, Moab and Edom were kept under control, and Syria was held in check.

3.) Next came the *Period of Syrian Ascendency* (B. C. 884-840). During the first two reigns of the House of Jehu Syria rose to great power tinder Hazael, and overran both Israel and Judah. At one time Israel was in danger of utter destruction, but was preserved. Near the close of these periods the dying prophecy of Elisha was uttered (2 Kings 13. 14-25).

4.) *The Period of Israelite Ascendency* (B. C. 840-772). Israel under Jeroboam II. took its turn of power, and for a brief period was again dominant to the Euphrates, as in the days of Solomon.

5.) *The Period of Assyrian Ascendency* (B. C. 772-721). But its glory soon faded away before that of Assyria, which was now rapidly becoming the empire of the East. Its rise meant the fall of Israel; and under the unfortunate Hoshea Samaria was taken, what was left of the ten tribes were carried captive, and the kingdom of Israel was extinguished (2 Kings 17. 1-6).

IV. **THE FATE OF THE TEN TRIBES.** There has been much idle discussion over this subject and some absurd claims set up; for example, that the Anglo-Saxon race are descended from the ten lost tribes—a statement opposed to all history, to ethnology, and to every evidence of language.

1. After their deposition nearly all the Israelites, having lost their national religion and having no bond of union, **mingled with the Gentiles** around them and lost their identity, just as hundreds of other races have done. The only bond which will keep a nation long alive is that of religion.

2. Some remained in Palestine, others returned thither and formed the **nucleus of the Samaritan people**, a race of mingled origin (2 Kings 17. 24-29).

3. Some of those who remained in the East retained their religion, or were revived in it, and later became a part of the **Jews of the dispersion**; though "the dispersion" was mainly Jewish, and not Israelite.

4. A few **families united with the Jews** returned with them to Palestine after the exile, yet retained their tribal relationship; for example, Anna (Luke 2. 36).

Blackboard Outline.

I. Cau. Div.   1. Opp. gov.   2. Opp. pro.   3. For. int.   4. Tri. jeal.   5. Am. Jer.   6. Fol. Re.

II. Res. Div.   1. Pol. res.   1.) Dis. emp.   2.) Riv. and weak.   3.) For. dom.
2. Rel. res.   1.) Pres. rel.   2.) Pro. rel.   3.) Conc. rel.

III. Kin. Isr.   1. Ext. 9,375.
2. Cap.   1.) Sh.   2.) Tir.   3.) Sam.
3. Rel.   1.) Wor. cal.   2.) Wor. Ba.   3.) Wor. Jeh.
4. Rul.   1.) Hou. Jer.   2.) Hou. Ra.   3.) Hou. Om.   4.) Hou. Je.   5.) Hou. Men.
5. For. Rel.   1.) Per. Div.   2.) Per. All.   3.) Per. Syr. Asc.   4.) Per. Isr. Asc.   5.) Per. Ass. Asc.

IV. Fat. Ten. Tri.   1. Min. Gen.   2. Sam. peo.   3. Disp.   4. Jews.

QUESTIONS FOR REVIEW.

What causes may be assigned for the division of Israel? How far was Solomon's government responsible? What was the relation of the prophets to the revolution? What foreign intrigues contributed to break up the kingdom? Who were connected with these intrigues? What ancient jealousy aided, and how? What man led in the breaking up of the kingdom? Whose folly enabled the plot to succeed?

What were the political results of the division? What were its religious results? How was this event from the Lord?

How long did the new kingdom of Israel last? What was its extent? What were its three successive capitals? What three forms of religion were found in it? Who was the first king of the ten tribes? What family introduced foreign idolatry? How many kings ruled over the ten tribes? What were the five royal houses? Which house raised Israel almost to its ancient power? What is this period of prosperity called? Who was the greatest King of Israel? With what other history is that of Israel interwoven? What were the five periods in the foreign relations of Israel? By what kingdom was Israel destroyed? Who was its last king? What finally became of the ten tribes?

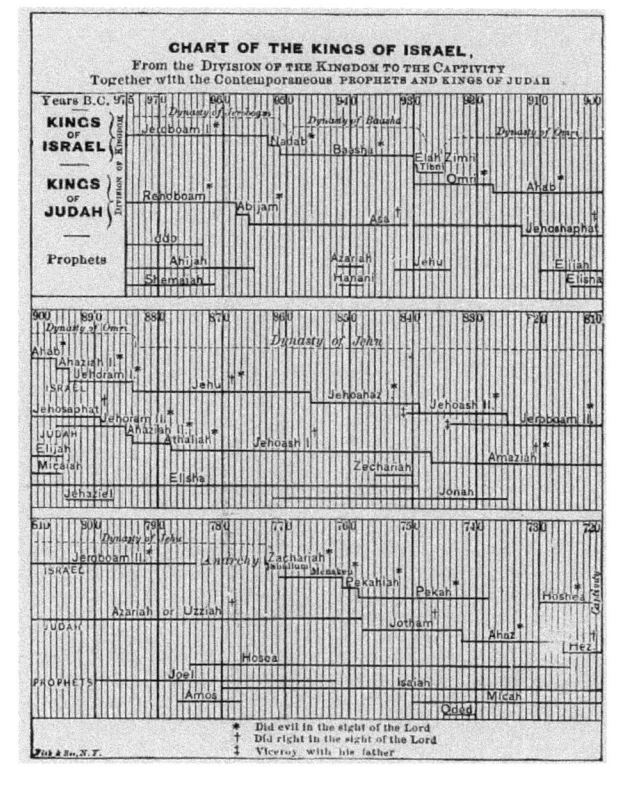

CHART OF THE KINGS OF ISRAEL,
From the DIVISION OF THE KINGDOM TO THE CAPTIVITY
Together with the Contemporaneous PROPHETS AND KINGS OF JUDAH

Subjects for Special Papers.

THE HISTORY AND TRAITS OF THE TRIBE OF EPHRAIM.
SHECHEM, AND EVENTS CONNECTED WITH IT.
THE RELIGION OF THE TEN TRIBES.
QUEEN JEZEBEL AND HER INFLUENCE.
THE MISSION OF ELIJAH.
ELISHA AND HIS INFLUENCE.

EIGHTH STUDY.
THE RIVAL THRONES—JUDAH.

I. GENERAL ASPECTS OF THE KINGDOM OF JUDAH.

1. **Its territory.** It embraced the mountain portion of the tribe of Judah, from the Dead Sea to the Philistine plain; a part of Benjamin, in which tribe the larger part of Jerusalem stood; and also a part of Dan (2 Chron. 11. 10). Simeon was nominally within its border, but was practically given up to the Arabians of the desert; Edom was tributary, though often in rebellion, and finally independent (1 Kings 22. 47; 2 Kings 8. 20); Philistia was outside of its boundary. Its extent was about 3,435 square miles, about half the area of Massachusetts.

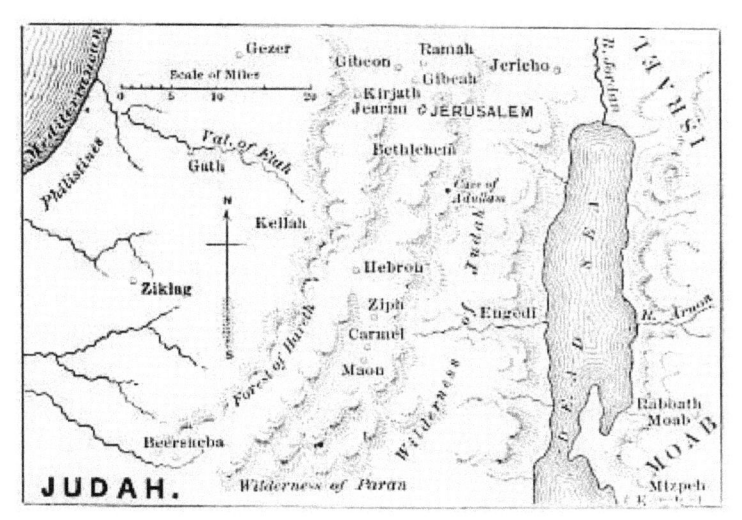

2. **Its government** was a monarchy, with but one family on the throne, the line of David, in direct succession, with the exception of Athaliah's usurpation (2 Kings 11. 1-3), through nineteen reigns.

3. **Its religion.** Through all the history we find two forms of worship strongly opposed to each other, yet both rooted in the nation. 1.) The worship of Jehovah through the temple, the priesthood, and the prophets. 2.) But side by side with this pure religion was the worship of idols upon "high places," probably begun as a form of worshiping Jehovah, but degenerating into gross and immoral idolatry. There was a struggle going on constantly between these two elements in the state, the spiritual and the

material. Notwithstanding the efforts of reforming kings like Jehoshaphat, Hezekiah, and Josiah, the general tendency was downward.

II. **THE DURATION OF THE KINGDOM.** The kingdom lasted from B. C. 975 to 587—more than one hundred and thirty years longer than Israel. Reasons for its endurance may have been:

1. **Its retired situation**: hemmed in by mountains and deserts; at a distance from the ordinary lines of travel; not in the direct path of conquest from any other nation. Judah had few foreign wars as compared with Israel.

2. **The unity of its people.** They were not ten tribes loosely connected, but one tribe, with a passionate love of their nation and a pride in their blood.

3. **Its concentration at Jerusalem.** Through all its history there was but one capital, where the palace of the king and the temple of the Lord were standing together.

4. **The reverence for the House of David** also kept the people together. There was no change in dynasty, and the loyalty of the people grew stronger through the generations toward the family on the throne. There being no usurpers, the throne was permanent until destroyed by foreign power.

5. **The purity of its religion** tended to keep the nation united, and to keep it in existence. No bond of self-interest or of blood will hold a people together as strongly as the tie of religion. Judah's strength was in the measure of her service of God, and when she renounced Jehovah her doom came speedily.

III. **PERIODS IN THE HISTORY.** Though Judah was not without political contact with other nations, yet its history is the record of internal events rather than external relations. We may divide its history into four epochs:

1. **The first decline and revival.** (B. C. 975-889.) 1.) The reigns of Rehoboam and Abijah marked a decline indicated by the Egyptian invasion and the growth of idolatry. 2.) The reign of Asa and Jehoshaphat showed a revival in reformation, progress, and power. Under Jehoshaphat Judah was at the height of prosperity. This was the time of peace with Israel, and of strength at home and abroad (2 Chron. 17. 5; 20. 30).

2. **The second decline and revival.** (B. C. 889-682.) 1.) For nearly two hundred years after the death of Jehoshaphat the course of Judah was downward. Edom was lost under Jehoram (2 Chron. 21. 8); the Baalite idolatry was introduced by the usurping queen, Athaliah (2 Kings 11. 18); the land was again and again invaded under Joash and Amaziah, and

Jerusalem itself was taken and plundered. 2.) But a great reformation was wrought under Hezekiah, who was the best and wisest of the kings of Judah, and the kingdom again rose to power, even daring to throw off the Assyrian yoke and defy the anger of the mightiest king then on the earth. At this time came the great event of the destruction of the Assyrian host (2 Kings 19. 30).

3. **The third decline and revival.** (B. C. 682-610.) 1.) The reforms of Hezekiah were short lived, for his son Manasseh was both the longest in reigning and the wickedest of the kings, and his late repentance did not stay the tide of corruption which he had let loose (2 Kings 21. 10-17; 2 Chron. 33. 1-18). The wickedness of Manasseh's reign was the great moral cause of the kingdom's destruction, for from it no reform afterward could lift the mass of the people. 2.) Josiah, the young reformer, attempted the task, but his efforts, though earnest, were only measurably successful, and after his untimely death the kingdom hastened to its fall (2 Kings 23. 29).

4. **The final decline and fall.** (B. C. 610-587.) 1.) The political cause of the destruction of the kingdom was the rise of Babylon. The old Assyrian empire went down about 625 B. C., and a struggle followed between Babylon and Egypt for the supremacy. Judah took the side of Egypt, which proved to be the losing side. 2.) After several chastisements and repeated rebellions Jerusalem was finally destroyed by Nebuchadnezzar, King of Babylon, and the kingdom of Judah was extinguished, B. C. 587.

Blackboard Outline.

I. Gen. Asp. Kin. Jud.   1. Terr. Tri. Jud. 3,435 m.   2. Gov. mon.   3. Rel.   1.) Jeh.   2.) Idol.

II. Dur. Kin.   1. Ret. sit.   2. Un. peo.   3. Conc. Jer.   4. Rev. Ho. Dav.   5. Pur. rel.

III. Per. Hist.   1. Fir. dec. rev.   1.) Dec. Reho. Abi.   2.) Rev. As. Jehosh.
2. Sec. dec. rev.   1.) Dec. 200 y.   2.) Rev. Hez.
3. Thi. dec. rev.   1.) Dec. Man.   2.) Rev. Jos.
4. Fin. dec. fal.   1.) Ris. Bab.   2.) Des. Jer.

QUESTIONS FOR REVIEW.

What was embraced in the kingdom of Judah?
What was its area?
How was it governed?
What was its religion?
What was associated with the worship of Jehovah?

What was the religious tendency of the people?
How long did the kingdom of Judah last?
What were the causes of this duration?
What were the periods in its history?
Under what kings was the first decline?
Who led in a revival and reformation?
Who was the greatest of the kings of Judah?
What took place during the second decline?
Who was the usurping queen?
What did this queen try to do?
Who wrought the second great reformation?
What was the character of this king?
What great destruction of Judah's enemies took place at this time?
Which reign was both longest, wickedest, and most evil in its results?
Who attempted a third reformation?
What was the result of his endeavor?
What was the political cause of the fall of Judah?
By what nation and by what king was Jerusalem finally destroyed?

Subjects for Special Papers.

HISTORY OF THE TRIBE OF JUDAH.
THE HOUSE OF DAVID.
THE RELIGION OF JUDAH.
THE PROPHETS OF JUDAH.
ANCIENT JERUSALEM.
THE KINGDOM OF JUDAH IN RELATION TO EGYPT AND ASSYRIA.

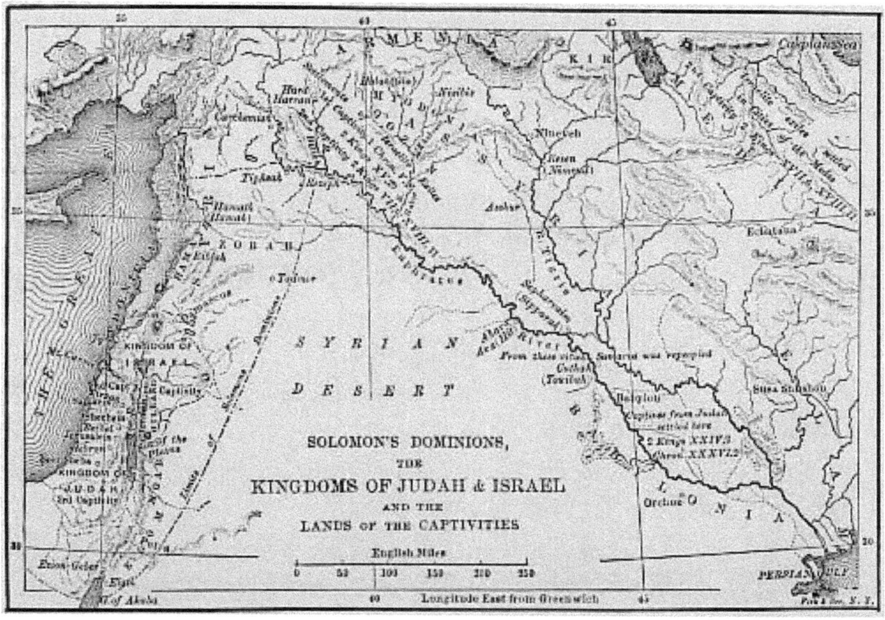
SOLOMON'S DOMINIONS,
THE
KINGDOMS OF JUDAH & ISRAEL
AND THE
LANDS OF THE CAPTIVITIES
English Miles
0 50 100 150 200 250
Longitude East from Greenwich
S Y R I A N
D E S E R T
Caspian Sea
Nineveh
Babylon
Ecbatana
Susa Shushan
Euphrates
Tigris
Tadmor
Carchemish
Tiphsah
Nisibis
Ashur
KINGDOM OF ISRAEL
KINGDOM OF JUDAH
Ezion-Geber
G. of Akaba

NINTH STUDY.
THE CAPTIVITY OF JUDAH.

I. We must distinguish between the **CAPTIVITY OF ISRAEL**, or the ten tribes, and **THAT OF JUDAH**.

1. The captivity of Israel took place B. C. 721, that of Judah B. C. 587. The southern kingdom lasted one hundred and thirty-four years longer than the northern.

2. Israel was taken captive by the Assyrians under Sargon; Judah by the Chaldeans under Nebuchadnezzar.

3. Israel was taken to the lands south of the Caspian Sea (2 Kings 17. 6); Judah to Chaldea, by the river Euphrates (Psa. 137. 1).

4. Israel never returned from its captivity, which was the end of its history; but Judah was brought back from its captivity and again became a flourishing state, though subject to foreign nations during most of its after history.

II. There were **THREE CAPTIVITIES** of Judah, all in one generation and all under one Chaldean king, Nebuchadnezzar:

1. **Jehoiakim's captivity.** (B. C. 607.) Jehoiakim was the son of Josiah, placed upon the throne after the battle of Megiddo, in which Josiah perished (2 Kings 23. 34). In the war between Pharaoh-nechoh of Egypt and Nebuchadnezzar (then joint king of Babylon with his father Nabopolassar) Jehoiakim, as a vassal of Nechoh, aided the Egyptians. After the defeat of Nechoh, Nebuchadnezzar marched to punish Jehoiakim. He was called away from the siege of Jerusalem by the death of his father and the necessity of hastening to Babylon to assume the government. Jehoiakim was spared, but a number of the nobles of Judah were taken to Babylon, perhaps as hostages for the king's good conduct. For three years Jehoiakim obeyed Nebuchadnezzar; then he rebelled, but was speedily reduced to subjection, and many of the leading people among the Jews were carried captive to Babylon (2 Kings 24. 1, 2). Among these captives was Daniel the prophet (Dan. 1. 1-6). From this event the *seventy years* of the captivity were dated (Jer. 27. 22; 29. 10), though the kingdom of Judah remained for twenty years longer. Jehoiakim, the king, was not taken away, though bound in chains for that purpose (2 Chron. 36. 6); he reigned several years after this event, but under suspicion of the Chaldeans, and his end was ignoble (Jer. 22. 18, 19; 36. 30).

2. **Jehoiachin's captivity.** (B. C. 598.) Jehoiachin was the son of Jehoiakim (called Jeconiah, 1 Chron 3. 16; Jer. 24. 1; and Coniah, Jer. 22. 24). He reigned only three months, and was then deposed by Nebuchadnezzar and carried to Babylon. With the young king and the royal family were taken thousands of the people of the middle classes, whom the land could ill spare (2 Kings 24. 8-16). Among these captives was Ezekiel, the prophet-priest (Ezek. 1. 1-3).

3. **Zedekiah's captivity.** (B. C. 587.) He was the uncle of Jehoiachin, and the son of the good Josiah (2 Kings 24. 17), and had been made king by Nebuchadnezzar. But he too rebelled against his master, to whom he had taken a solemn oath of fidelity (2 Chron. 36. 13). The Chaldeans were greatly incensed by these frequent insurrections, and determined upon a final destruction of the rebellious city. After a long siege Jerusalem was taken, and the king was captured while attempting flight. He was blinded and carried away to Babylon, the city was destroyed, and nearly all the people left alive were also taken to the land of Chaldea (2 Kings 25. 1-11). After this captivity the city lay desolate for fifty years, until the conquest of Babylon by Cyrus (B. C. 536).

III. Let us ascertain the **CAUSES OF THE CAPTIVITY**; why the Jews were taken up bodily from their own land and deported to a distant country.

1. Such deportations were a frequent **policy of Oriental conquerors**. The Orientals had three ways of dealing with a conquered people: that of extermination or wholesale butchery, which is frequently described upon the Assyrian monuments; that of leaving them in the land under tribute, as subjects of the conqueror; and that of deporting them *en masse* to a distant land. Frequently, when the interests of the empire would be served by changing the population of a province, this plan was carried out. Thus the ten tribes were carried to a land near the Caspian Sea, and other people were brought to Samaria in their place (2 Kings 17. 6, 24). A similar plan with respect to Judah was proposed by Sennacherib (2 Kings 18. 31, 32), but was thwarted by the destruction of the Assyrian host.

2. We have already noticed another cause of the captivity in the frequent **rebellions of the kings of Judah** against the authority of Babylon. The old spirit of independence, which had made Judah the leader of the twelve tribes, was still strong, and it was fostered by the hope of universal rule, which had been predicted through centuries, even while the kingdom was declining. The prophets, however, favored submission to Babylon; but the nobles urged rebellion and independence. Their policy was pursued, and the unequal strife was taken up more than once. The rebellions always failed; but after several attempts the patience of Nebuchadnezzar was

exhausted, and the destruction of the rebellious city and the deportation of the population was ordered.

3. But underneath was another and a deeper cause—in **the rivalry of Egypt and Babylon**. Whenever in history one nation has been dominant there has been another nation, next in strength, as its rival to check its supremacy. Thus Greece stood in the way of Persia, Carthage in the way of republican Rome, and Parthia in the way of imperial Rome. In the earlier days Assyria (and after Assyria Babylon) was the controlling power in the East; but it was always opposed by Egypt, which, though less powerful, was yet strong enough to be dangerous to Assyrian or Chaldean supremacy. Palestine stood on the border of the Assyrian Empire toward Egypt; and in Palestine there were two parties, the Assyrian and the Egyptian; one counseling submission to Assyria, the other seeking alliance with Egypt against Assyria (Isa. 31. 1-3; 37. 6). After Babylon took the place of Nineveh the Chaldean party took the place of the Assyrian, as the Chaldean Empire was the successor of the Assyrian Empire. The prophets, led by Jeremiah, always counseled submission to Babylon, and warned against trusting to Egypt, which had never given any thing more than promises; but the nobles were of the Egyptian party, and constantly influenced the kings to renounce the yoke of Babylon, and to strike for independence by the aid of Egypt. Under Egyptian influence the later kings of Judah made attempt after attempt to rebel against the Chaldean Empire. But the expected help from Egypt never came, and Judah was left again and again to suffer the wrath of Babylon (Jer. 37. 5-9). The necessity of making the frontier of the Chaldean Empire safe on the side toward Egypt was the political cause for the deportation of the tribe of Judah. Nebuchadnezzar dared not to leave a people on the soil who would constantly endanger the entrance to his dominions by plotting with the Egyptians. He therefore took up the Jews bodily, placed them in the center of his empire, and turned the land of Judah into a desolation.

4. There was underlying all these political reasons a moral cause in **the divine purpose to discipline the nation**. The captivity was a weeding-out process, to separate the precious from the vile, the false from the true, the "remnant" from the mass. There had always been two distinct elements in Israel and Judah—the spiritual, God-fearing few, and the worldly, idol-worshiping many. The worldly and irreligious took part in the resistance to the King of Babylon; and the worshipers of Jehovah, led by the prophets, urged submission. As a result, the nobles and the warriors, for the most part, perished; while the better part, the strength and hope of the nation, were carried away captive. Notice that the captives were mainly of the middle class, the working element (2 Kings 24. 14-16). Those who had submitted to the Chaldeans were also taken away (2 Kings 25. 11). The

prophet expressed greater hope for those taken away than for those left behind (Jer. 24. 1-10). The captives were the root of Judah, out of which in due time a new nation should rise.

IV. **THE CONDITION OF THE CAPTIVES IN CHALDEA** was far better than we are apt to suppose.

1. They received **kind treatment**; were regarded not as slaves or prisoners, but as colonists. At a later captivity by the Romans the Jews were sold as slaves and dispersed throughout the empire. Such wholesale enslavement was common after a conquest. For some reason the Chaldeans did not enslave the Jews at the time of their conquest, but colonized them as free people. This may have been because the captives as a class were of the "Chaldean party" among the Jews, and hence were treated in a measure as friends. The letter of Jeremiah to the exiles (Jer. 29. 1-7) shows that they were kindly dealt with in Chaldea. Some of them were received at the court and rose to high station in the realm (Dan. 1. 1-6).

2. **Their organization was maintained.** The exiles were not merged into the mass of the people where they were living, but retained their own system, and were recognized as a separate colony. Their dethroned kings had a semi-royal state, and at death an honorable burial (Jer. 52. 31-34; 34. 4, 5). The captives were governed by elders, rulers of their own nation (Ezek. 8. 1; 14. 1; 20. 1). Such a system is still pursued in the East, where the government is according to race as well as according to locality; that is, the different races in one province will each have separate rulers. There was a "prince of Judah" at the close of the captivity (Ezra 1. 8). This fact of a national organization was a fortunate one for the exiles. If they had been dispersed as slaves throughout the empire, or even had been scattered as individuals, they would soon have been merged among the Gentiles, and would have lost their identity as a people. But maintaining as a separate race, and in Jewish communities, they were readily gathered for a return to their own land when the opportunity came.

3. **Their law and worship were observed.** There were no sacrifices, for these could be offered only at Jerusalem in the temple. But the people gathered for worship and for the study of the law far more faithfully than before the exile; for adversity is a school of religious character far more than prosperity. The exile would naturally exert an influence in the direction of religion. While the irreligious and idolatrous among the captives would soon drop out of the nation and be lost among the Gentiles, the earnest, the spiritual, and the God-fearing would grow more intense in their devotion. The institutions which date from the captivity (noticed below, under "Results of Captivity") are an evidence of this fact.

4. **They were instructed by prophets and teachers.** Jeremiah lived for some time after the beginning of the captivity, made a visit to Babylon, and wrote at least one letter to the exiles (Jer. 13. 4-7; 29. 1-3). Daniel lived during the captivity, and, though in the court, maintained a deep interest in his people, and comforted them by his prophecies. Ezekiel was himself one of the captives, and all his teachings were addressed to them (Ezek. 1. 1-3). Many evangelical and eminent Bible scholars are of the opinion that the latter part of Isaiah, from the fortieth chapter to the end, was given by a "later Isaiah" during the exile; but whether written at that time or earlier, it must have circulated among the captives and given them new hope and inspiration. The radical change in the character of the Jews which took place during this period shows that a great revival swept over the captive people and brought them back to the earnest religion of their noblest ancestors.

5. **Their literature was preserved and enlarged.** Internal evidence shows that the Books of the Kings were finished and the Books of the Chronicles written at this time or soon afterward; the Books of Daniel, Ezekiel, Habakkuk, and other of the minor prophets were given; and a number of the best psalms were composed during this epoch, as such poems are likely to be written in periods of trial and sorrow. Out of the many psalms we cite Psalms 124, 126, 129, 130, 137, as manifestly written during the captivity. The exile was an age of life and vigor to Hebrew literature.

V. **THE RESULTS OF THE CAPTIVITY.** In the year 536 B. C. the city of Babylon was taken by Cyrus, King of the combined Medes and Persians. One of his first acts was to issue an edict permitting the exiled Jews to return to their own country and rebuild their city. Not all the Jews availed themselves of the privilege, for many were already rooted in their new homes, where they had been for two generations. But a large number returned (Ezra 2. 64), and re-established the city and state of the Jews. The captivity, however, left its impress upon the people down to the end of their national history, and even to the present time.

1. **There was a change in language**, from Hebrew to Aramaic or Chaldaic. The books of the Old Testament written after the restoration are in a different language from the earlier writings. After the captivity the Jews needed an interpreter in order to understand their own earlier Scriptures. Allusion to this fact is given in Neh. 8. 7. The Chaldee of Babylon and the Hebrew were sufficiently alike to cause the people during two generations to glide imperceptibly from one to the other, until the knowledge of their ancient tongue was lost to all but the scholars.

2. **There was a change in habits.** Before the captivity the Jews were a secluded people, having scarcely any relation with the world. The captivity brought them into contact with other nations, and greatly modified their manner of living. Hitherto they had been mostly farmers, living on their own fields; now they became merchants and traders, and filled the world with their commerce. Rarely now do we find a Jew who cultivates the ground for his support. They are in the cities, buying and selling. This tendency began with the Babylonian captivity, and has since been strengthened by the varied experiences, especially by the persecutions of the Jews during the centuries.

3. **There was a change in character.** This was the most radical of all. Before the captivity the crying sin of Judah, as well as of Israel, was its tendency to idolatry. Every prophet had warned against it and rebuked it; reformers had risen up; kings had endeavored to extirpate, but all in vain; the worshipers of God were the few, the worshipers of idols were the many. After the captivity there was a wonderful transformation. From that time we never read of a Jew bowing his knee before an idol. The entire nation was a unit in the service of Jehovah. Among all the warnings of the later prophets, and the reforms of Ezra and Nehemiah, there is no allusion to idolatry. That crime was utterly and forever eradicated; from the captivity until to-day the Jews have been the people of the one, invisible God, and intense in their hatred of idols. We may not know all the causes of this change, but some of them were: 1.) The fact that the idolatrous element largely perished, and the spiritual element formed the bulk of the captives. 2.) The idol-worshipers among the captives would naturally be less loyal to the national ideas, and would more readily assimilate with the heathen; while the religious among the exiles would grow all the more devoted to their religion as their only hope in trial. 3.) The most ardent lovers of their country and their religion would be the most eager to return after the exile; hence, the new state was founded by zealous Jews, who gave it religious spirit. So in modern times the spirit of the Pilgrims and the Puritans gave tone to New England, and through New England to America.

4. **There were new institutions** as the result of the captivity. Two great institutions arose during the captivity:

1.) The *synagogue*, which grew up among the exiles, was carried back to Palestine, and was established throughout the Jewish world. This was a meeting of Jews for worship, for reading the law, and for religious instruction. It had far greater influence than the temple after the captivity; for while there was but one temple in all the Jewish world, there was a synagogue in every city and village where Jews lived; and while the temple was the seat of a priestly and ritualistic service, the synagogue promoted freedom of religious thought and utterance. Out of the synagogue, far more than the temple, grew the Christian Church.

2.) *The order of scribes* was also a result of the captivity. The days of direct inspiration through prophets were passing away, and those of the written Scripture, with a class of men to study and interpret it, came in their place. During the captivity the devout Jews studied the books of their literature, the law, the psalms, the histories, and the prophets. After the captivity arose a series of scholars who were the expounders of the Scriptures. Their founder was Ezra, at once a priest, a scribe, and a prophet (Ezra 7. 1-10), who arranged the books and in a measure completed the canon of Old Testament Scripture.

5. **There was a new hope, that of a Messiah.** From the time of the captivity the Jewish people looked forward with eager expectation to the coming of a Deliverer, the Consolation of Israel, the "Anointed One" (the word Messiah means "anointed"), who should lift up his people from the dust, exalt the throne of David, and establish an empire over all the nations. This had been promised by prophets for centuries before the exile, but only then did it begin to shine as the great hope of the people. It grew brighter with each generation, and finally appeared in the coming of Jesus Christ, the King of Israel.

6. From the captivity there **were two parts of the Jewish people**; the Jews of Palestine, and the Jews of the dispersion. 1.) The Jews of Palestine, sometimes called Hebrews (Acts 6. 1), were the lesser in number, who lived in their own land and maintained the Jewish state. 2.) The Jews of the dispersion were the descendants of those who did not return after the decree of Cyrus (Ezra 1. 1), but remained in foreign lands and gradually formed Jewish "quarters" in all the cities of the ancient world. They were the larger in number, and later were called "Grecian Jews," or Hellenists, from the language which they used (Acts 6. 1). Between these two bodies there was a close relation. The Jews of the dispersion had synagogues in every city (Acts 15. 1), were devoted to the law, made constant pilgrimages to Jerusalem, and were recognized as having one hope with the Jews of Palestine. The traits of the two bodies were different, but each contributed its own element toward the making of a great people.

Blackboard Outline.

I. Cap. Isr. Jud. 1. Isr. 721. Jud. 587. 2. Ass. Sar.—Chal. Neb. 3. Cas. Sea.—Riv. Eup. 4. Nev. ret.—Bro. b.

II. Thr. Cap. Jud. 1. Jeh. cap. 607. 2. Jehn. cap. 598. 3. Zed. cap. 587.

III. Caus. Cap. 1. Pol. Or. conq. 2. Reb. kgs. Jud. 3. Riv. Eg. Bab. 4. Div. pur. dis.

IV. Con. Cap. 1. Kin. tre. 2. Org. main. 3. La. wor. obs. 4. Ins. pro. tea. 5. Lit. pre. enl.

V. Res. Cap. 1. Ch. lan. 2. Ch. hab. 3. Ch. char. 4. Ne. ins. (syn. scr.) 5. Hop. Mess. 6. Two. par. peo.

QUESTIONS FOR REVIEW.

From what earlier captivity must that of Judah be distinguished?
What were the dates of these two captivities?
By whom was each nation taken captive?
Where was each nation carried captive?
What followed the captivity in each nation?
What were the three captivities of Judah?
What were the events of the first captivity of Judah?
Who were carried away at this time?
What date is connected with this captivity?
What were the events of the second captivity of Judah?
Who were then taken away?
What were the events of the third captivity?
How long was Jerusalem left in ruins?
By whom, and when, were the Jews permitted to return from captivity?
What causes may be assigned for the carrying away of the Jews?
What were the customs of ancient Oriental conquerors?
How did the conduct of the kings of Judah bring on the captivity?
What rivalry between nations was a cause of the captivity?
What were the two parties in the kingdom of Judah?
How was the carrying away of the Jews a political necessity?
What was the moral cause of the captivity?

How were the captive Jews treated?
What evidences show that their national organization was continued during the captivity?
Why was this fact a fortunate one for the exiles?
What customs of the Jews were observed during the captivity?
What instructors did the Jews have during this period?
What was the condition of Jewish literature during the captivity?
What events followed the decree of Cyrus?
Did all the exiles of the Jews return?
What change in language was wrought by the captivity?
What change in habits followed the captivity?
What great change in religion came as the result of the captivity?
How can that change be accounted for?
What two institutions arose during the captivity?
What new hope arose at this time?
How were the Jews divided after the captivity?

Subjects for Special Papers.

THE GREAT ORIENTAL EMPIRES.
THE CITY OF BABYLON.
THE PROPHETS OF THE CAPTIVITY.
THE PSALMS OF THE CAPTIVITY.
THE REIGN OF NEBUCHADNEZZAR.
THE FALL OF BABYLON.

TENTH STUDY.
THE JEWISH PROVINCE.

From the return of the exiles, B. C. 536, to the final destruction of the Jewish state by the Romans, A. D. 70, the history of the chosen people is closely interwoven with that of the East in general. During most of this time Judea was a subject province, belonging to the great empires which rose and fell in succession. For a brief but brilliant period it was an independent state, with its own rulers. As most of this period comes between the Old and New Testaments its events are less familiar to Bible readers than the other portions of Israelite history. We therefore give more space than usual to the facts, only selecting the most important, and omitting all that have no direct relation with the development of the divine plan in the Jewish people.

I. The history divides itself into **FOUR PERIODS**, as follows:

1. **The Persian period**, B. C. 536 to 330, from Cyrus to Alexander, while the Jewish province was a part of the Persian Empire. Very few events of these two centuries have been recorded, but it appears to have been a period of quiet prosperity and growth. The Jews were governed by their high-priests under the general control of the Persian government. The principal events of this period were:

1.) *The second temple.* (B. C. 535-515.) This was begun soon after the return from exile (Ezra 3. 1, 2, 8), but was not completed until twenty-one years afterward (Ezra 6. 15, 16). It was smaller and less splendid than that of Solomon, but was built upon the same plan.

2.) *Queen Esther's deliverance.* (B. C. 474.) This took place, not in Judea, but in Shushan (Susa), the capital of the Persian Empire. The king referred to as Ahasuerus was probably Xerxes, and the events of Esther's elevation and intercession took place after the defeat of his invasion of Greece. The whole story is in accord with both Persian customs and the character of Xerxes.

3.) *Ezra's reformation.* (B. C. 450.) The coming to Jerusalem of Ezra the scribe was a great event in Israelite history; for, aided by Nehemiah, he led in a great reformation of the people. He found them neglecting their law and following foreign customs. He awakened an enthusiasm for the Mosaic law, aroused the patriotism of the people, and renewed the ancient faith. His work gave him the title of "the second founder of Israel."

4.) *The separation of the Samaritans.* (B. C. 409.) For the origin of the Samaritans, see 2 Kings 17. 22-34. They were a mingled people, both in race and religion; but until the captivity were permitted to worship in the temple at Jerusalem. After the return from Babylon the Samaritans and the Jews grew further and further apart. The Samaritans opposed the rebuilding of the temple (Ezra 4. 9-24), and delayed it for many years; and a century later strove to prevent Nehemiah from building the wall of Jerusalem (Neh. 4. 2). Finally they established a rival temple on Mount Gerizim, and thenceforth the two races were in bitter enmity (John 4. 9).

5.) *The completion of the Old Testament canon.* The prophets after the restoration were Haggai, Zechariah, and Malachi; but the author of most of the latest books was Ezra, who also arranged the Old Testament nearly, perhaps fully, in its present form. Thenceforward no more books were added, and the scribe or interpreter took the place of the prophet.

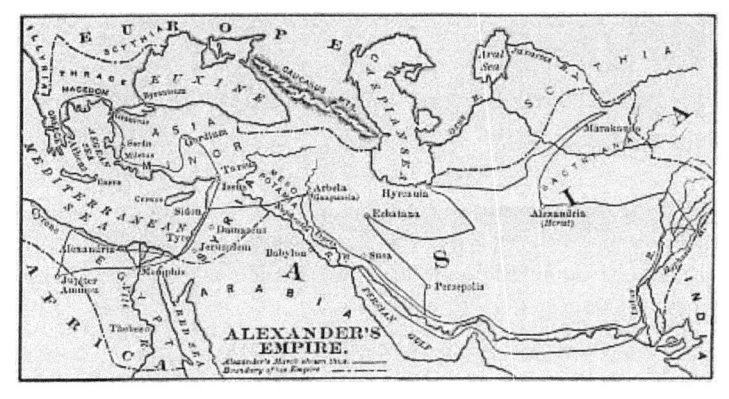

ALEXANDER'S EMPIRE.

2. **The Greek period.** (B. C. 330-166.) In the year 330 B. C. Alexander the Great won the empire of Persia in the great battle of Arbela, by which the sovereignty of the East was transferred from Asia to Europe, and a new chapter in the history of the world was opened. Alexander died at the hour when his conquests were completed, and before they could be organized and assimilated; but the kingdoms into which his empire was divided were all under Greek kings, and were all Greek in language and civilization. Judea was on the border between Syria and Egypt, and belonged alternately to each kingdom. We divide this period into three subdivisions.

1.) *The reign of Alexander.* (B. C. 330-321.) The Jews had been well treated by the Persian kings and remained faithful to Darius, the last King of Persia, in his useless struggle. Alexander marched against Jerusalem, determined to visit upon it heavy punishment for its opposition, but (according to tradition) was met by Jaddua, the high-priest, and turned from an enemy to a friend of the Jews.

2.) *The Egyptian supremacy.* (B. C. 311-198.) In the division of Alexander's conquests Judea was annexed to Syria, but it soon fell into the hands of Egypt, and was governed by the Ptolemies (Greek kings of Egypt) until 198 B. C. The only important events of this period were the rule of Simon the Just, an exceptionally able high-priest, about 300 B. C., and the translation of the Old Testament into the Greek language for the use of the Jews of Alexandria, who had lost the use of Hebrew or Chaldee. This translation was made about 286 B. C., according to Jewish tradition, and is known as the Septuagint version. It was regarded as an act of sacrilege by the Palestinian Jews to translate their Holy Scriptures into the language of heathens, and for centuries the anniversary of the completion of the Septuagint was observed as a day of humiliation and prayer.

3.) *The Syrian supremacy.* (B. C. 198-166.) About the year 198 B. C. Judea fell into the hands of the Syrian kingdom, also ruled by a Greek dynasty, the Seleucidæ, or descendants of Seleucus. This change of rulers brought to the Jews a change of treatment. Hitherto they had been permitted to live undisturbed upon their mountains, and to enjoy a measure of liberty, both in civil and ecclesiastical matters. But now the Syrian kings not only robbed them of their freedom, but also undertook to compel them to renounce their religion by one of the most cruel persecutions in all history. The temple was desecrated and left to ruin, and the worshipers of Jehovah were tortured and slain, in the vain endeavor to introduce the Greek and Syrian forms of idolatry among the Jews. Heb. 11, 33-40, is supposed to refer to this persecution. When Antiochus, the Syrian king, found that the Jews could not be driven from their faith, he deliberately determined to exterminate the whole nation. Uncounted thousands of Jews were slaughtered, other thousands were sold as slaves, Jerusalem was well nigh destroyed, the temple was dedicated to Jupiter Olympius, and the orgies of the Bacchanalia were substituted for the Feast of Tabernacles. The religion of Jehovah and the race of the Jews seemed on the verge of utter annihilation in their own land.

3. **The Maccabean period.** (B. C. 166-40.) But the darkest hour precedes the day; the cruelties of the Syrians caused a new and splendid epoch to rise upon Israel.

1.) *The revolt of Mattathias.* In the year 170 B. C. an aged priest, Mattathias, unfurled the banner of independence from the Syrian yoke. He did not at first aim for political freedom, but religious liberty; but after winning a few victories over the Syrian armies he began to dream of a free Jewish state. He died in the beginning of the war, but was succeeded by his greater son, Judas Maccabeus.[I]

2.) *Judas Maccabeus* gained a greater success than had been dreamed at the beginning of the revolt. Within four years the Jews recaptured Jerusalem and reconsecrated the temple. (The anniversary of this event was ever after celebrated in the Feast of Dedication, John 10. 22.) Judas ranks in history as one of the noblest of the Jewish heroes, and deserves a place beside Joshua, Gideon, and Samuel as a liberator and reformer.

3.) *The Maccabean dynasty.* Judas refused the title of king, but his family established a line of rulers who by degrees assumed a royal state, and finally the royal title. In the year 143 B. C. Jewish liberty was formally recognized, and the Maccabean princes ruled for a time over an independent state. Between 130 and 110 B. C. Edom, Samaria, and Galilee were added to Judea. The latter province had been known as "Galilee of the Gentiles" (Isa. 9. 1); but by degrees the foreigners withdrew, and the province was occupied by Jews who were as devoted and loyal as those of Jerusalem.

4.) *The rise of the sects.* About B. C. 100 the two sects, or schools of thought, the Pharisees and Sadducees, began to appear, though their principles had long been working. The Pharisees ("separatists") sought for absolute separation from the Gentile world and a strict construction of the law of Moses, while the Sadducees ("moralists") were liberal in their their theories and in their lives.

4. **The Roman period.** (B. C. 40-A. D. 70.) It is not easy to name a date for the beginning of the Roman supremacy in Palestine. It began in B. C. 63, when Pompey the Great (afterward the antagonist of Julius Cæsar) was asked to intervene between two claimants for the Jewish throne, Hyrcanus and Aristobulus. Pompey decided for Hyrcanus, and aided him by a Roman army. In his interest he besieged and took Jerusalem, and then placed Hyrcanus in power, but without the title of king. From this time the Romans were practically, though not nominally, in control of affairs.

1.) *Herod the Great.* We assign as the date of the Roman rule 40 B. C., when Herod (son of Antipater, an Edomite, who had been the general of Hyrcanus) received the title of king from the Roman Senate. From this time Palestine was regarded as a part of the Roman Empire. Herod was the ablest man of his age, and one of the most unscrupulous. He ruled over all Palestine, Idumea (ancient Edom), and the lands south of Damascus.

2.) *Herod's temple.* Herod was thoroughly hated by the Jews, less for his character than for his foreign birth. To gain their favor he began rebuilding the temple upon a magnificent scale. It was not completed until long after his death, which took place at Jericho about the time when Jesus Christ, the true King of the Jews, was born (Matt. 2. 1, 2).

3.) *The tetrarchies.* By Herod's will his dominions were divided into four tetrarchies ("quarter-rulings," a title for a fourth part of a kingdom). Three of these were in Palestine—Archelaus receiving Judea, Idumea, and Samaria; Antipas (the Herod of Luke 4. 19, 20; 23. 7-11) receiving Galilee and Perea; and Philip (Luke 3. 1) having the district of Bashan. About A. D. 6 Archelaus was deposed, and a Roman, Coponius, was appointed the first Procurator of Judea, which was made a part of the prefecture of Syria. The rest of Jewish annals belongs properly to the New Testament history.

II. Through these periods we notice the gradual **PREPARATION FOR THE GOSPEL**, which was steadily advancing.

1. **There was a political preparation.** Six centuries before Christ the world around the Mediterranean was divided into states, whose normal condition was war. At no time was peace prevalent over all the world at once. If Christ had come at that time it would have been impossible to establish the Gospel except through war and conquest. But kingdoms were absorbed into empires, empires rose and fell by turns, each with a larger conception of the nation than its predecessor. From the crude combination of undigested states in the Assyrian Empire to the orderly, assimilated, systematic condition of the Roman world was a great advance. Christ appeared at the only point in the world's history when the great nations of the world were under one government, with a system of roads such that a traveler could pass from Mesopotamia to Spain and could sail the Mediterranean Sea in perfect safety.

2. **There was a preparation of language.** The conquests of Alexander, though accomplished in ten years, left a deeper impress upon the world than any other two centuries of history. They gave to the whole of that world one language, the noblest tongue ever spoken by human lips, "a language fit for the gods," as men said. Through Alexander Greek cities were founded every-where in the East, Greek kingdoms were established, the Greek literature and the Greek civilization covered all the lands. That was the language in which Paul preached the Gospel, and in which the New Testament was written—the only language of the ancient world in which the thoughts of the Gospel could be readily expressed. While each land had its own tongue, the Greek tongue was common in all lands.

3. While these preparations were going on there was another in progress at the same time, **the preparation of a race**. We might point to the history of the Israelites from the migration of Abraham as a training; but we refer now to their special preparation for their mission after the restoration, B. C. 536. There was a divine purpose in the division of Judaism into two streams; one a little fountain in Palestine, the other a river dispersed over all the lands. Each branch had its part in the divine plan. One was to concentrate its energies upon the divine religion, to study the sacred books, to maintain a chosen people, whose bigotry, narrowness, and intolerance kept them from destruction; the other branch was out in the world, where every Jewish synagogue in a heathen city kept alive the knowledge of God, and disseminated that knowledge, drawing around it the thoughtful, spiritual minds who were looking for something better than heathenism. Palestine gave the Gospel, but the Jews of the dispersion carried it to the Gentiles, and each synagogue in the foreign world became the nucleus of a Christian Church, where for the first time Jew and Gentile met as equals.

4. Finally, there was the **preparation of a religion**. The Gospel of Christ was not a new religion; it was the new development of an old religion. As we study the Old Testament we see that each epoch stands upon a higher religious plane. There is an enlargement of spiritual vision between Abraham and Moses; between Moses and David; between David and Isaiah; between Isaiah and John the Baptist. Pharisee and Sadducee each held a share of the truth which embraced the best thought of both sects. The work of many scribes prepared the way for the coming of the Lord, and just when revelation was brought up to the highest level, when a race was trained to apprehend and proclaim it, when a language had been created and diffused to express it, when the world was united in one great brotherhood of states, ready to receive it—then, in the fullness of times, the Christ was manifested, who is over all, God blessed forever.

Blackboard Outline.

I. Four Per. 1. Per. per. 1.) Sec. tem. 2.) Q. Es. del. 3.) Ez. ref. 4.) Sep. Sam. 5.) Com. O. T. can.
2. Gk. per. 1.) Rei. Alex. 2.) Eg. sup. 3.) Syr. sup.
3. Macc. per. 1.) Rev. Mat. 2.) Jud. Macc. 3.) Macc. dyn. 4.) Ri. sec.
4. Rom. per. 1.) Her. Cr. 2.) Her. tem. 3.) Tetr.

II. Prep. Gosp. 1. Pol. prep. 2. Prep. lan. 3. Prep. rac. 4. Prep. rel.

QUESTIONS FOR REVIEW.

With what history is that of the Jews interwoven during this period?
What was the political condition of the Jews at this time?
What are the four periods of this history?
Who were the rulers of the Jews during the first period?
What building was erected after the return from captivity?
What great deliverance was effected by a woman?
What great reforms were effected by a scribe?
What title has been given to him?
What were the events connected with the separation of the Samaritans?
Who were the prophets of the restoration?
By whom was the Old Testament canon arranged?
What brought on the Greek period?
What events of Jewish history were connected with Alexander the Great?
Under what people did the Jews fall afterward?
What were the events of the Egyptian rule?
What is the Septuagint?
How was its translation regarded by the Jews of Palestine?
In what kingdom, after Egypt, did Judea fall?

How was it governed by its new masters?
Who instituted a great persecution?
What was the effect of this persecution?
Who led the Jews in revolt?
What great hero arose at this time?
What line of rulers arose in his family?
What was the growth of the Jewish state at this time?
What sects of the Jews arose?
How did Judea fall under the Roman power?
Whom did the Romans establish as king?
What were his dominions?
What building did he erect?
How was his kingdom divided after his death?
What finally became of Judea?

Subjects for Special Papers.

CYRUS THE EMANCIPATOR.
THE CONQUESTS OF ALEXANDER.
JUDAS MACCABEUS.
THE JEWISH SECTS.
HEROD THE GREAT.
THE JEWS OF THE DISPERSION.

FOOTNOTES:

[1] The origin of this title is obscure. Some regard it as meaning "the hammer," like a similar name in the Middle Ages, Charles Martel. Others say that it was a part of the Hebrew inscription on the banner of Judas, "Micamo Ka Baalim Jehovah," "Who is like unto thee among the gods, O Jehovah?" Still others that it was made up as a sort of charm from the last letters of the words Abraham, Isaac, Jacob. The Maccabean princes were also called Asmoneans.

www.ingramcontent.com/pod-product-compliance
Ingram Content Group UK Ltd.
Pitfield, Milton Keynes, MK11 3LW, UK
UKHW042151281224
453045UK00004B/316

9 789364 732918